HAL•LEONARD®
GUITAR PLAY-ALONG

AUDIO
ACCESS
INCLUDED

PLAYBACK+
Speed • Pitch • Balance • Loop

FLEETWOOD MAC

CONTENTS

To access audio visit:
www.halleonard.com/mylibrary

1557-0782-1330-4548

PHOTOGRAPH BY BRIAN SNYDER, CAMERA PRESS LONDON.

ISBN 978-1-4768-0855-0

7777 W. BLUEMOUND RD. P.O. BOX 13819 MILWAUKEE, WI 53213

Visit Hal Leonard Online at
www.halleonard.com

The Chain

**Words and Music by Stevie Nicks, Christine McVie,
Lindsey Buckingham, Mick Fleetwood and John McVie**

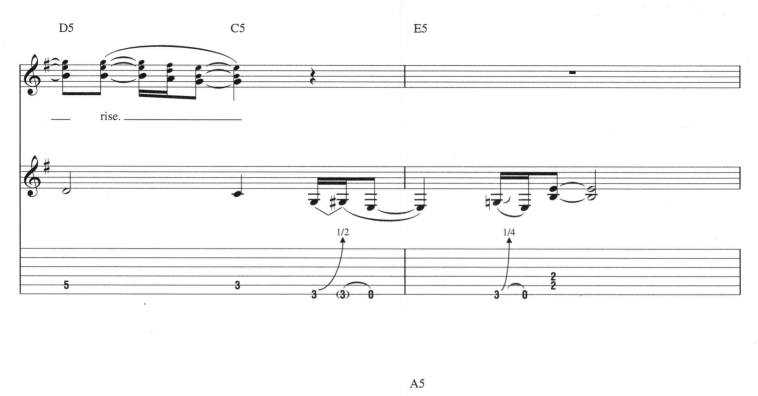

rise.

Run in the shad - ows; _____ damn your love, damn your lies. _

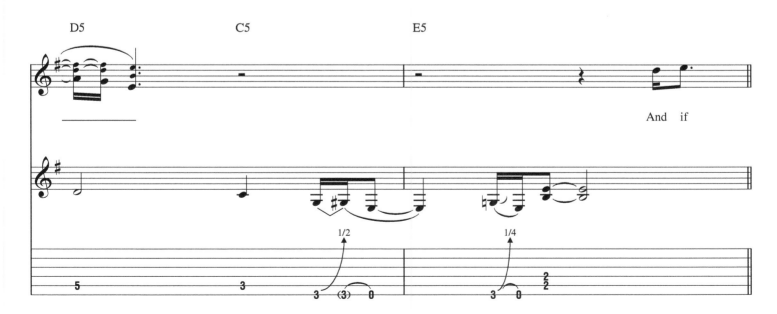

And if

Chorus

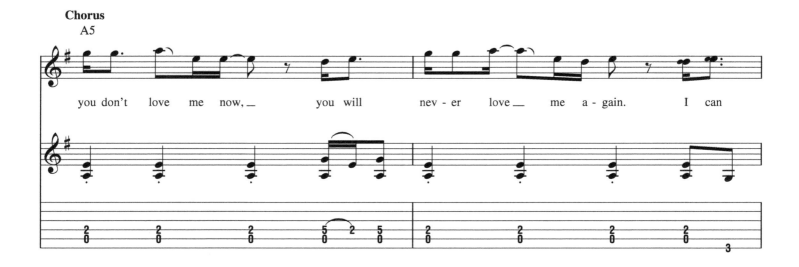

you don't love me now, __ you will nev - er love __ me a - gain. I can

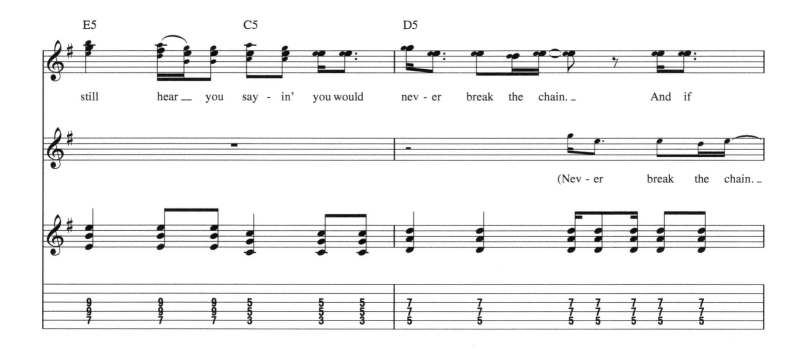

still hear __ you say - in' you would nev - er break the chain. __ And if

(Nev - er break the chain. __

you don't love me now, __ you will nev - er love __ me a - gain. I can

__ You don't love me now... __

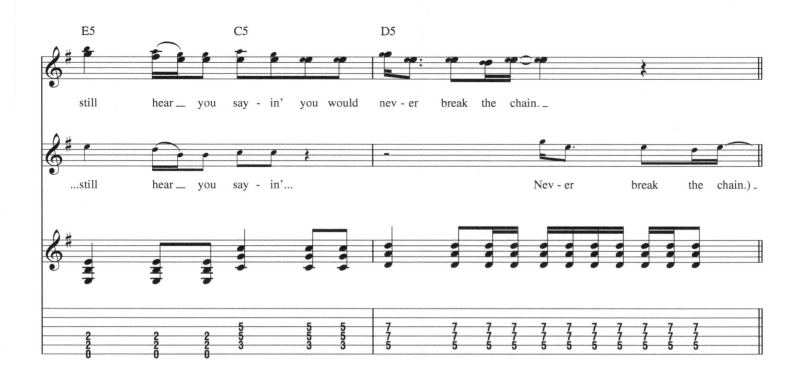

still hear — you say - in' you would nev - er break the chain. —

...still hear — you say - in'... Nev - er break the chain.) —

Interlude

Verse

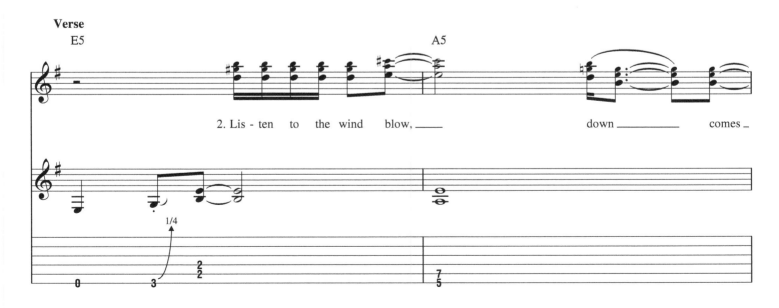

2. Lis - ten to the wind blow, _____ down _____ comes _

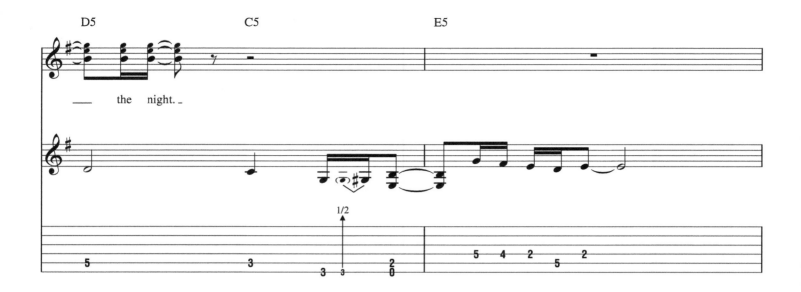

the night.

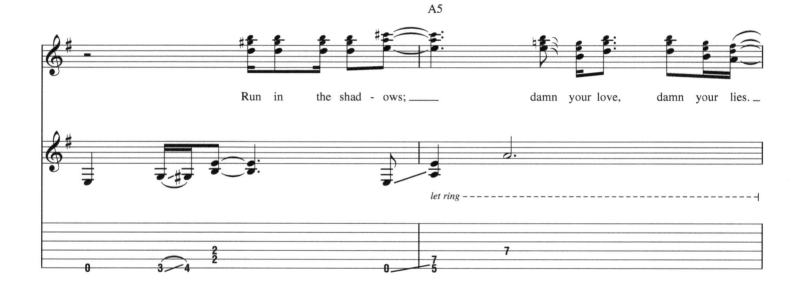

Run in the shad - ows; _____ damn your love, damn your lies. _

let ring -

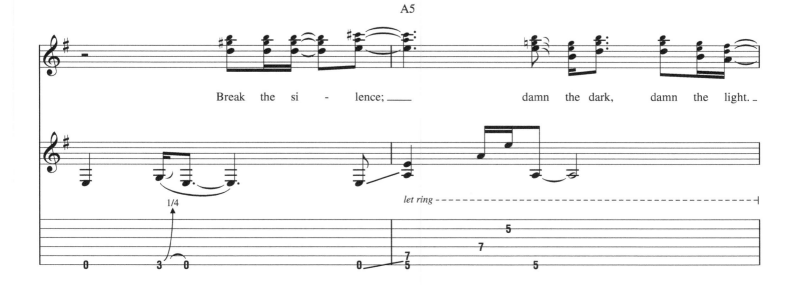

Break the si - lence; _____ damn the dark, damn the light. _

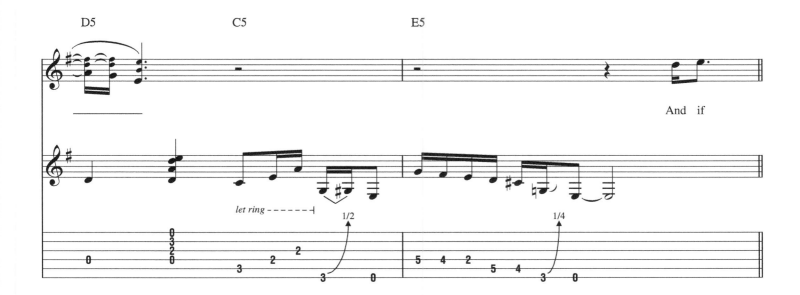

And if

Chorus

you don't love me now, _ you will nev - er love _ me a - gain. I can

still hear __ you say - in' you would nev - er break the chain. __ And if

(...still hear __ you say - in'... Nev - er break the chain. __

you don't love me now, __ you will nev - er love __ me a - gain. I can

__ You don't love me now... __

1/4

still hear __ you say - in' you would nev - er break the chain. __ And if

...still hear __ you say - in'... Nev - er break the chain. __

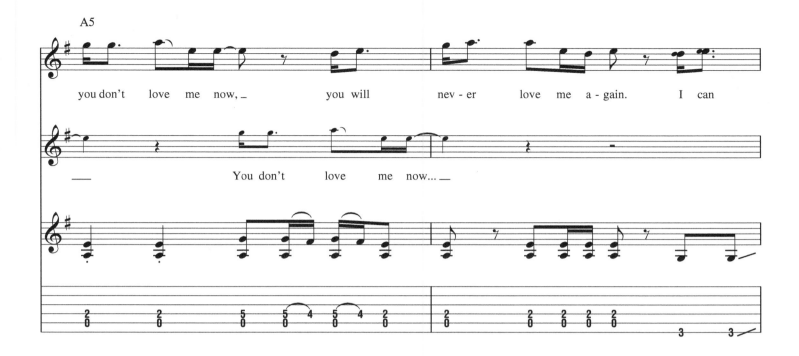

A5

you don't love me now, _ you will nev - er love me a - gain. I can

You don't love me now... _

E5   C5   D5

still hear _ you say - in' you would nev - er break the chain. _

...still hear _ you say - in'...   Nev - er break the chain.) _

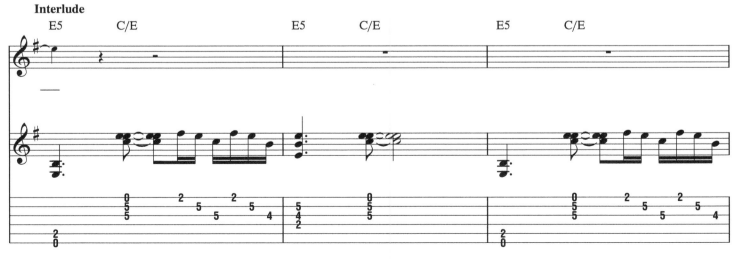

Interlude

E5 C/E   E5 C/E   E5 C/E

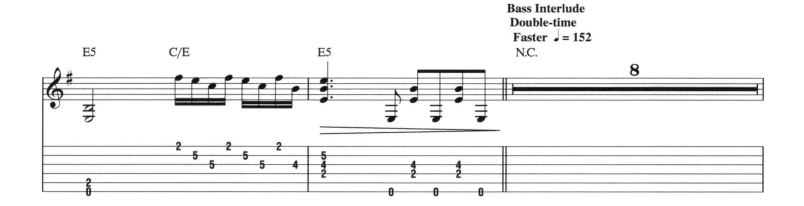

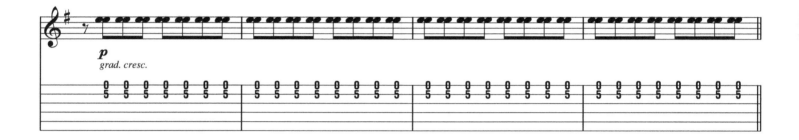

Guitar Solo

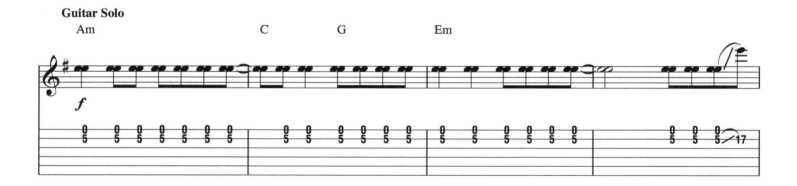

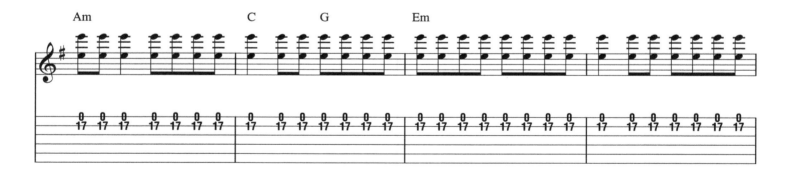

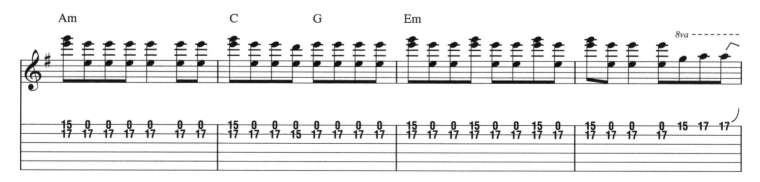

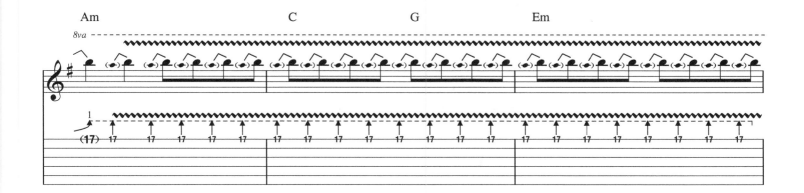

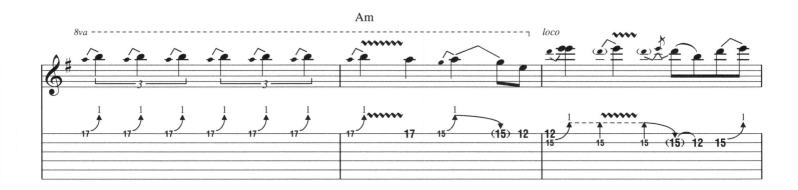

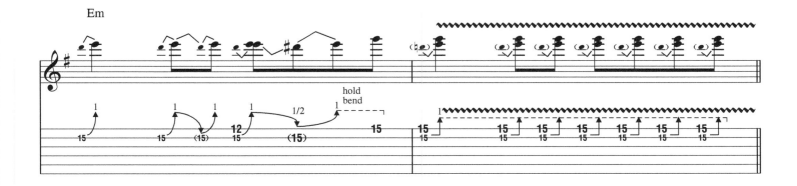

Outro-Chorus

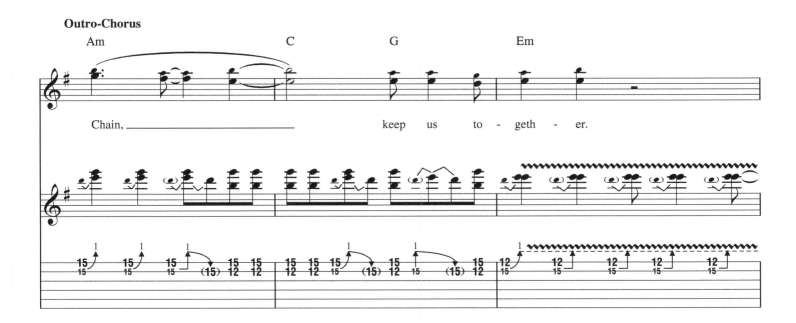

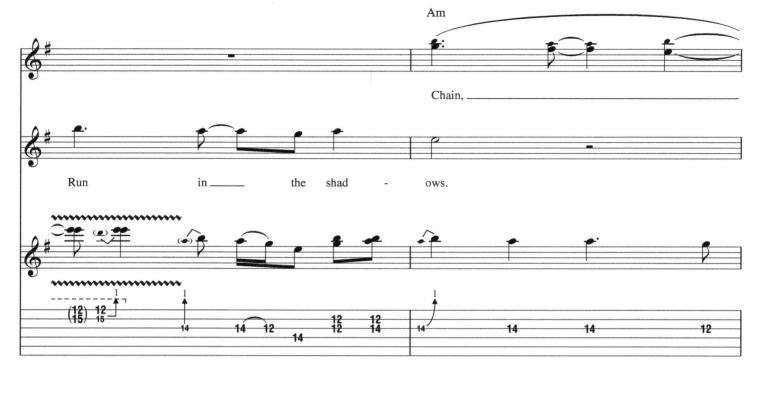

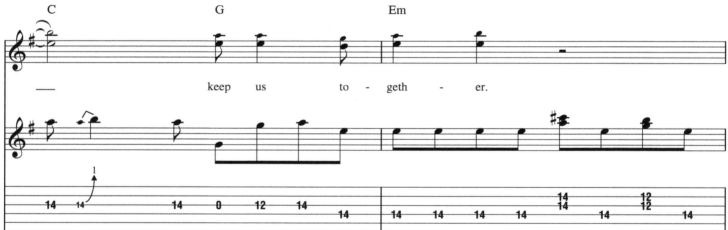

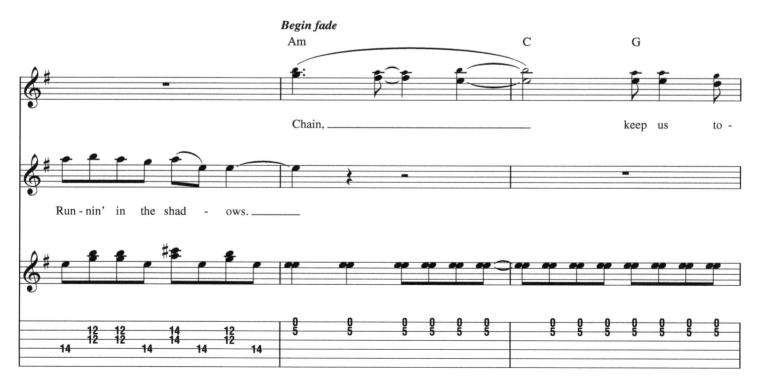

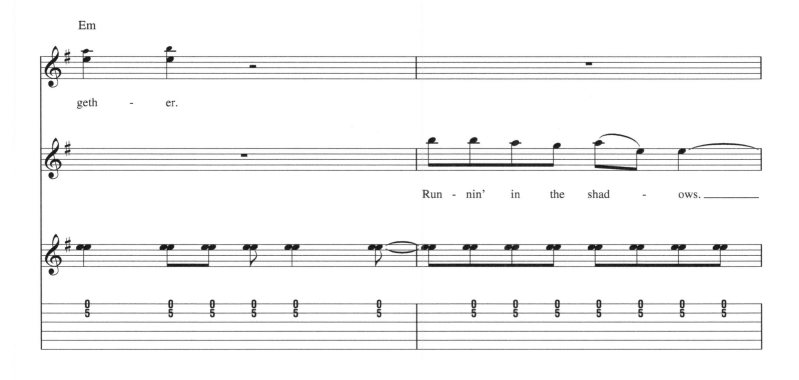

geth - er.

Run - nin' in the shad - ows. _____

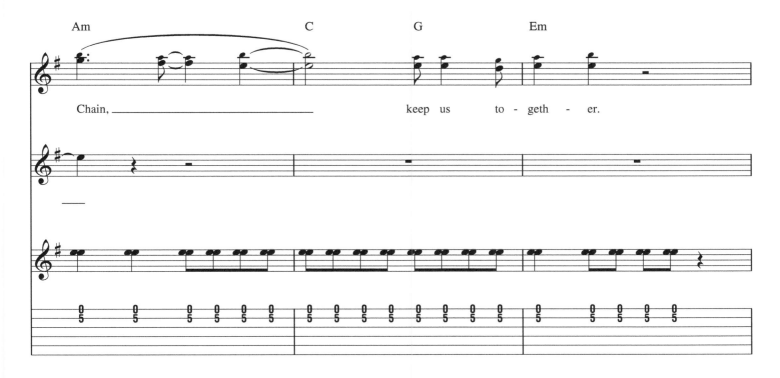

Chain, _____ keep us to - geth - er.

Fade out

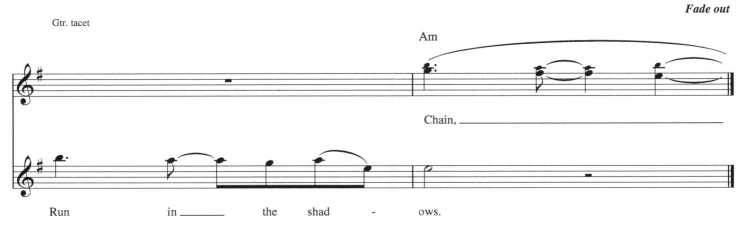

Gtr. tacet

Chain, _____

Run in _____ the shad - ows.

Don't Stop

Words and Music by Christine McVie

Chorus

Don't stop think - in' a-bout to-mor - row. Don't stop, it - 'll soon __ be here. __

It-'ll be _____ bet-ter than be-fore. __ Yes-ter-day's gone, __ yes - ter-day's gone. __

Interlude

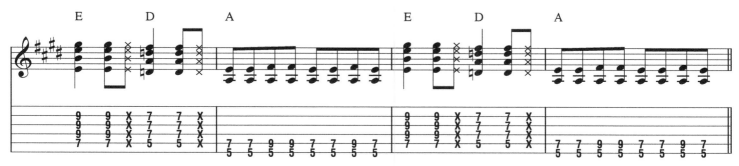

Verse

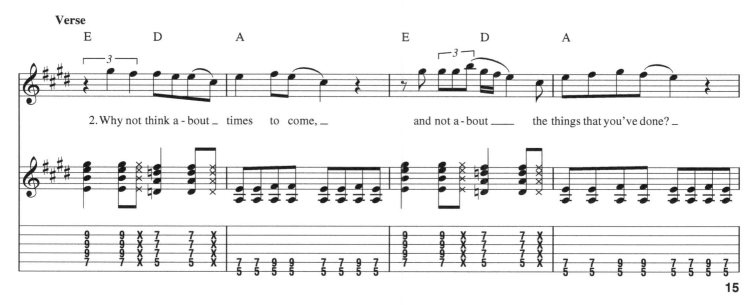

2. Why not think a - bout __ times to come, __ and not a-bout _____ the things that you've done? __

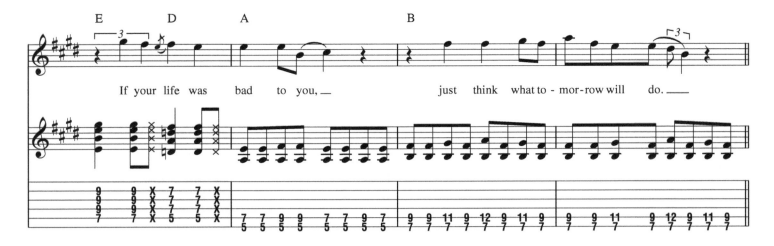

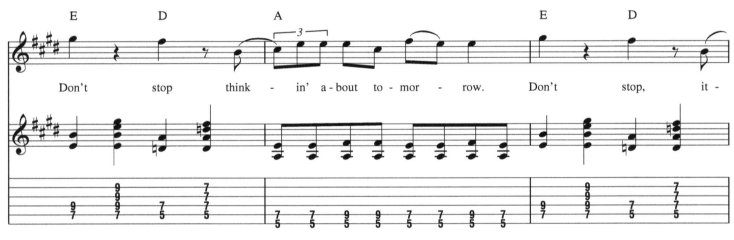

Chorus

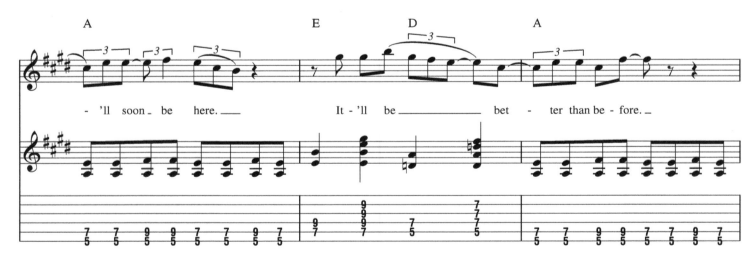

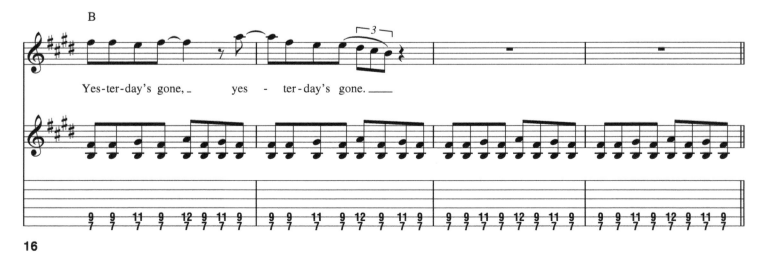

Guitar Solo

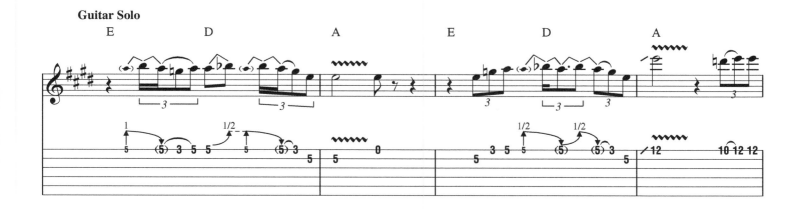

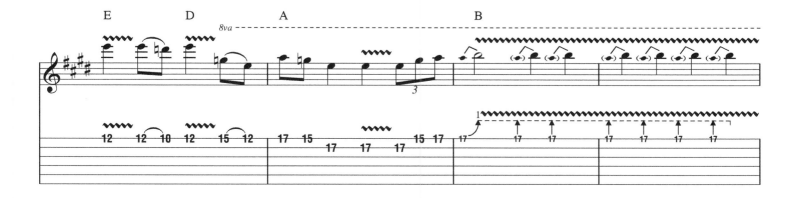

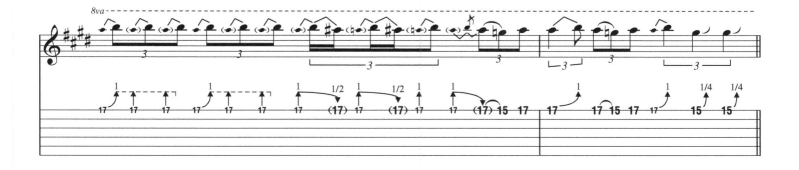

Verse

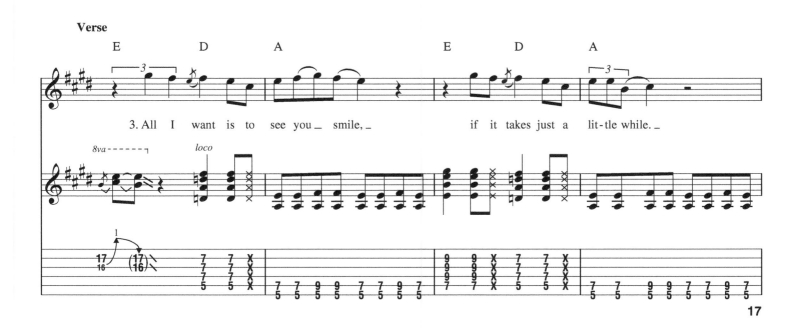

3. All I want is to see you __ smile, __ if it takes just a lit-tle while. __

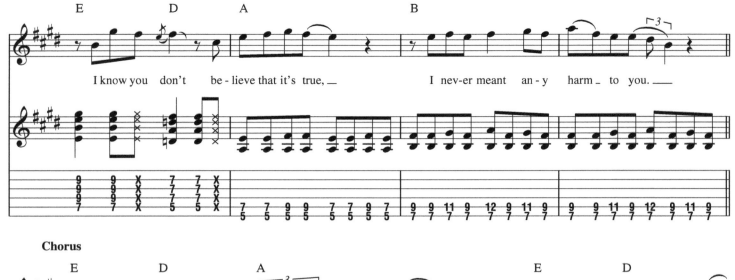

I know you don't be - lieve that it's true, __ I nev - er meant an - y harm __ to you. __

Chorus

Don't stop think - in' a - bout to - mor - row. Don't stop, it -

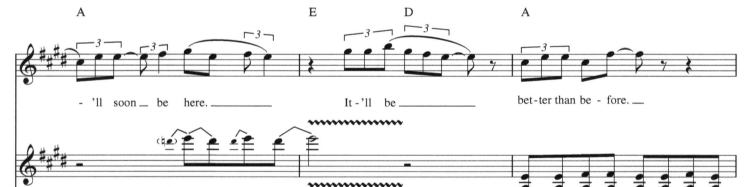

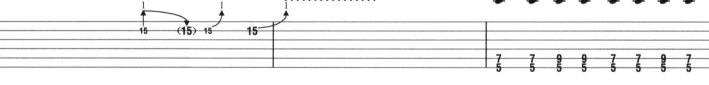

- 'll soon __ be here. _____ It -'ll be _____ bet - ter than be - fore. __

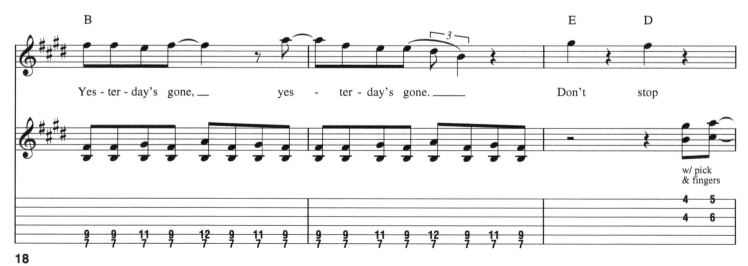

Yes - ter - day's gone, __ yes - ter - day's gone. _____ Don't stop

w/ pick
& fingers

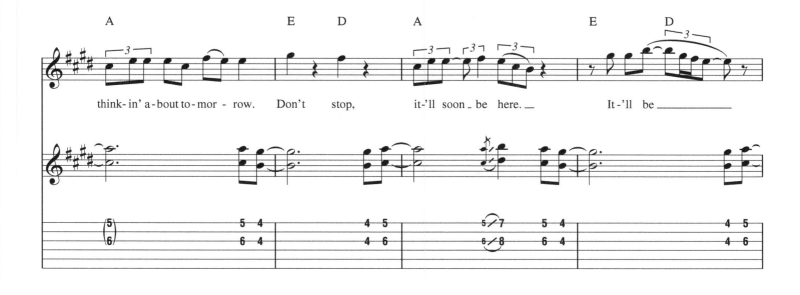

think-in' a-bout to-mor - row. Don't stop, it-'ll soon be here. It-'ll be

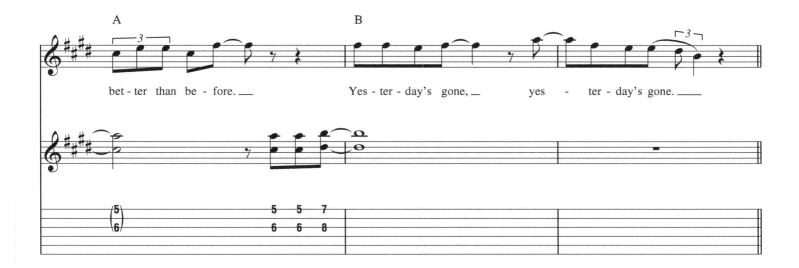

bet - ter than be - fore. Yes - ter - day's gone, yes - ter-day's gone.

Outro

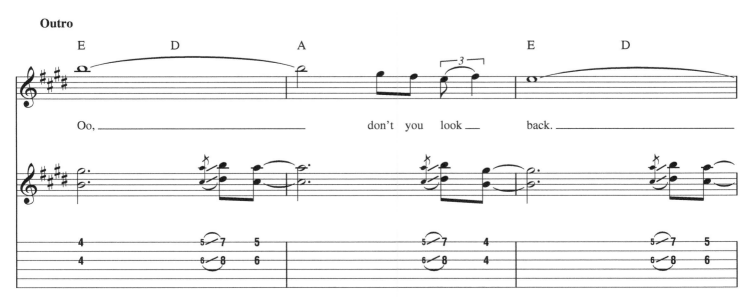

Oo, don't you look back.

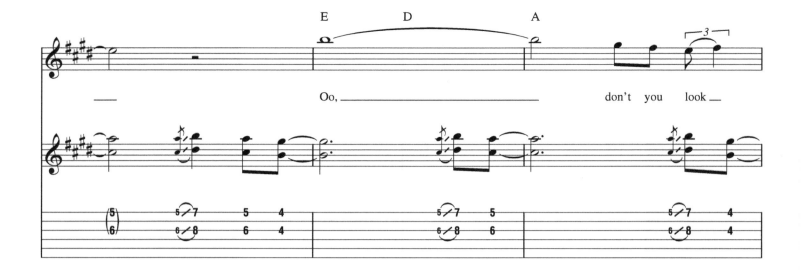

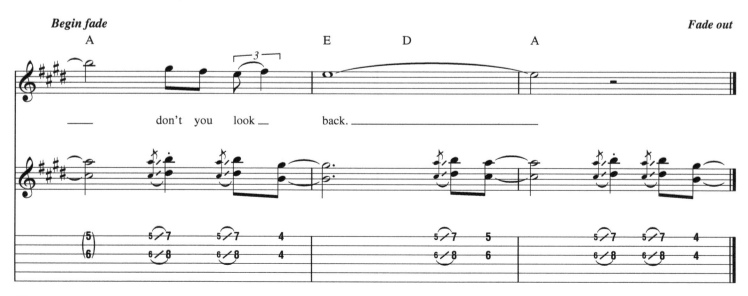

Dreams

Words and Music by Stevie Nicks

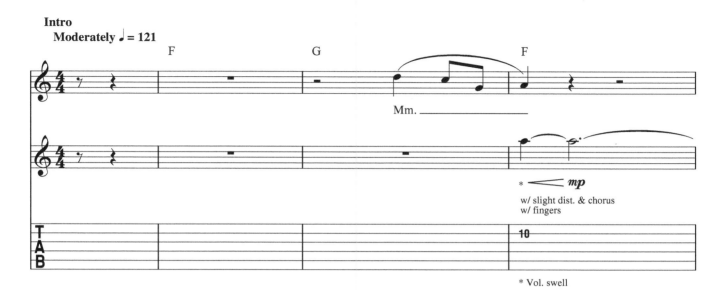

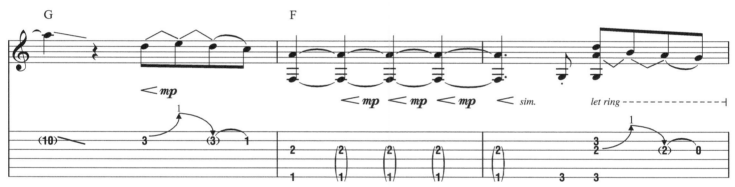

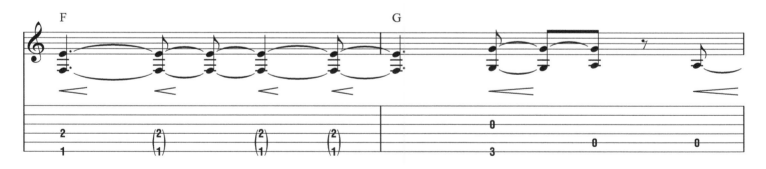

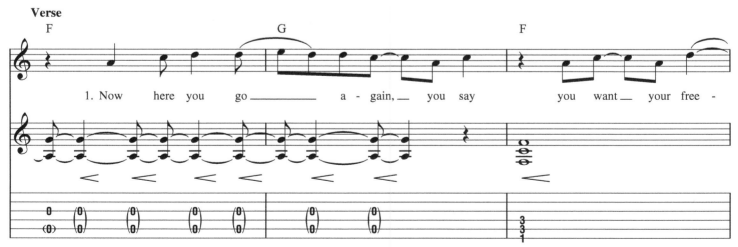

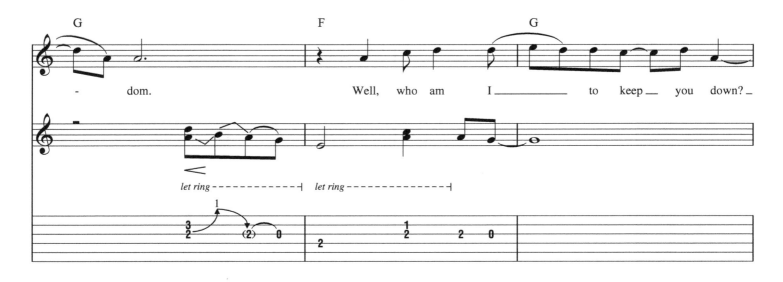

- dom.　　Well,　who　am　I＿＿＿＿　to　keep＿　you　down?＿

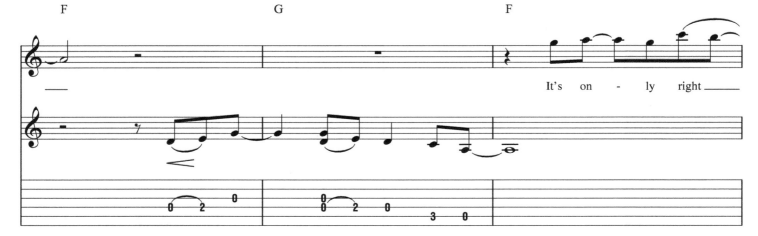

＿　　　　It's　on - ly　right＿＿＿

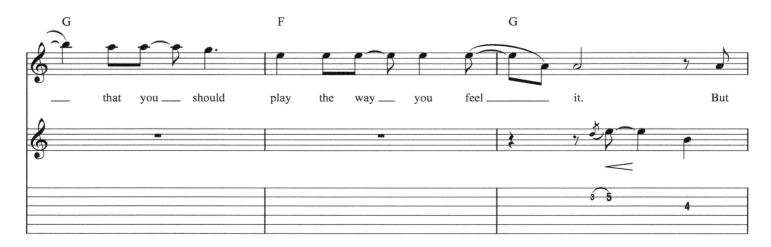

＿　that　you＿　should　play　the　way＿　you　feel＿＿＿＿　it.　　But

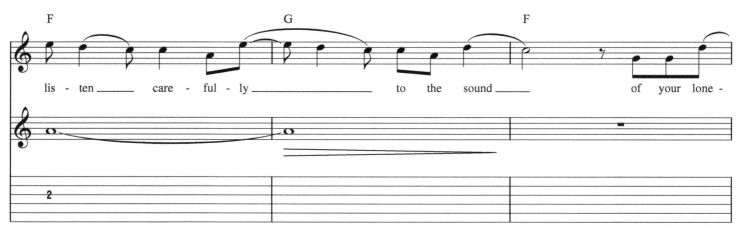

lis - ten＿＿＿　care - ful - ly＿＿＿＿＿＿　to　the　sound＿＿＿　　　　of　your　lone -

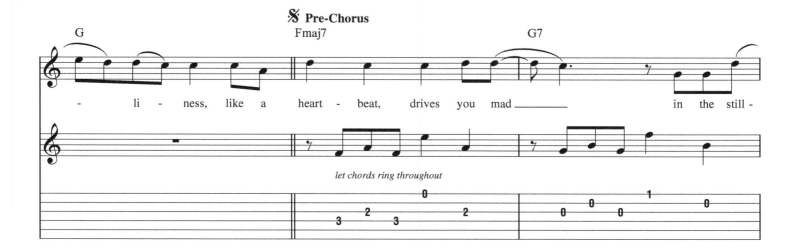

let chords ring throughout

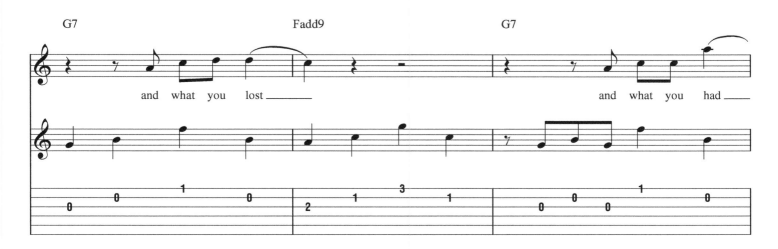

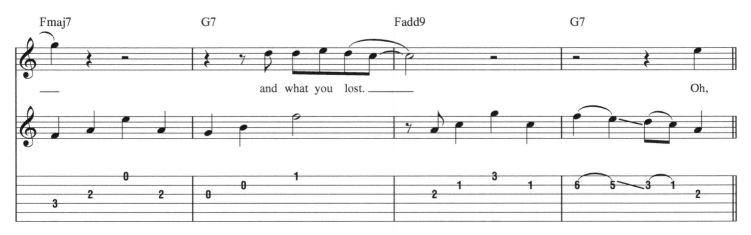

Chorus

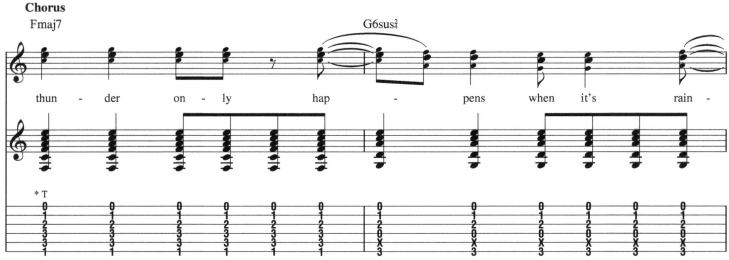

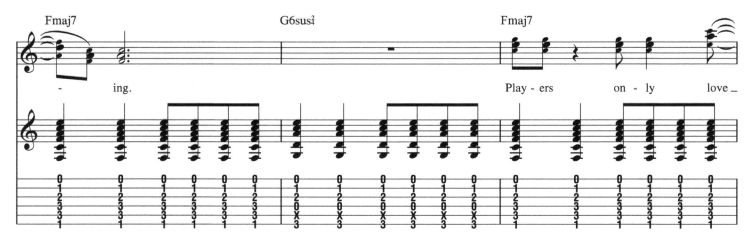

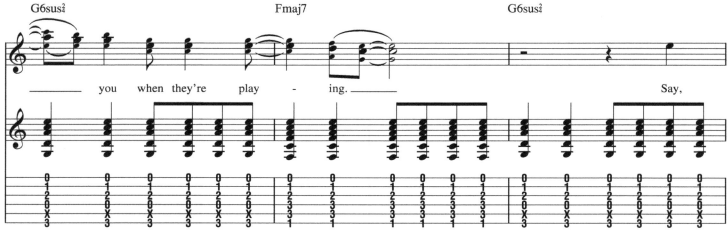

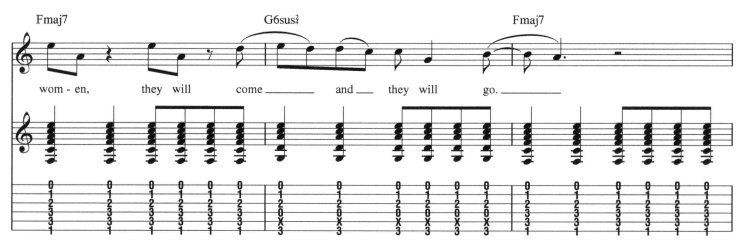

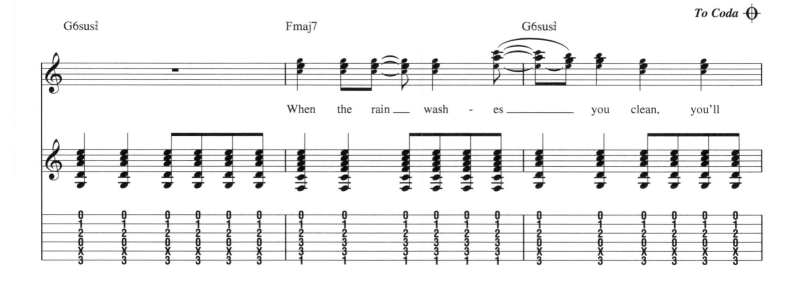

When the rain — wash - es ———— you clean, you'll

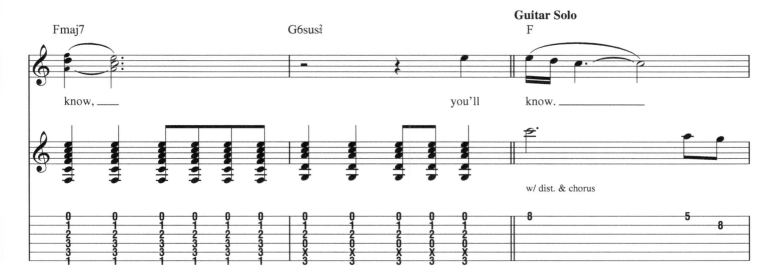

know, ——   you'll   know. ——————

Guitar Solo

w/ dist. & chorus

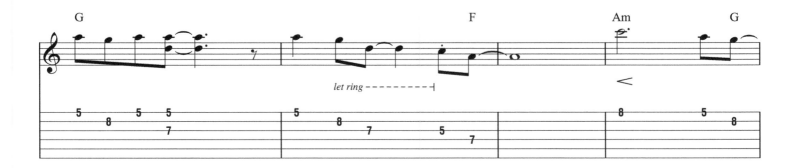

let ring - - - - - - - - -⌐

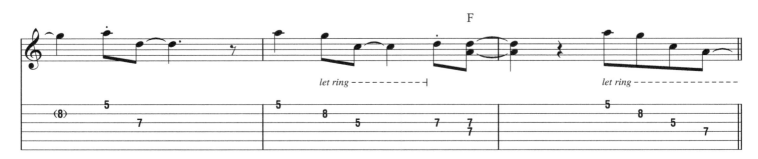

let ring - - - - - - - - - -⌐   let ring - - - - - - - - - - - - - -

Verse

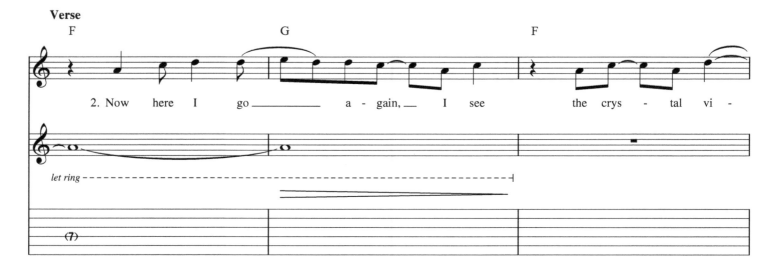

2. Now here I go _____ a - gain, ___ I see ___ the crys - tal vi -

- sion. I keep my vi - sions to my - self. ___

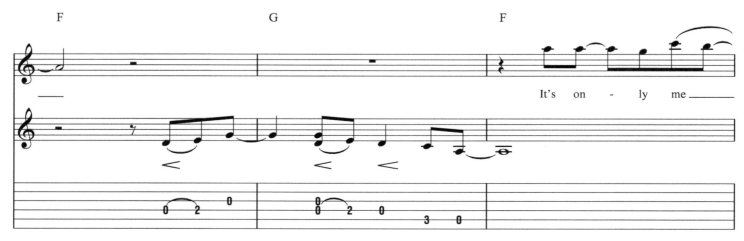

It's on - ly me ___

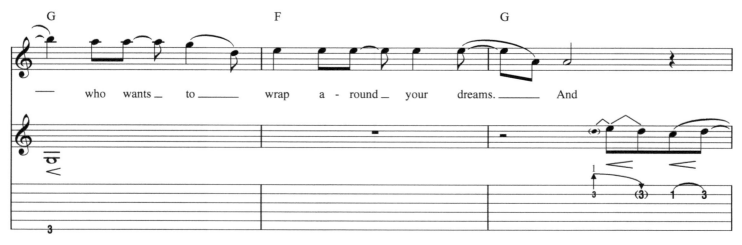

___ who wants ___ to _____ wrap a - round ___ your dreams. _____ And

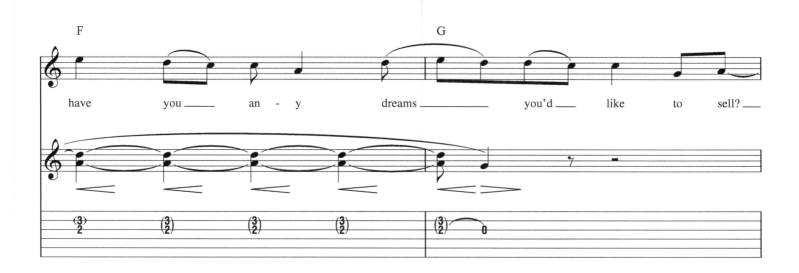

have you ___ an - y dreams _____ you'd ___ like to sell? ___

Gtr. tacet

D.S. al Coda

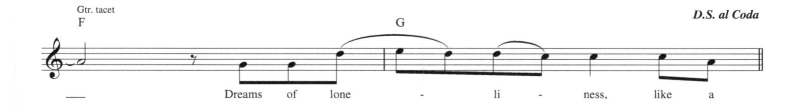

___ Dreams of lone - li - ness, like a

Coda

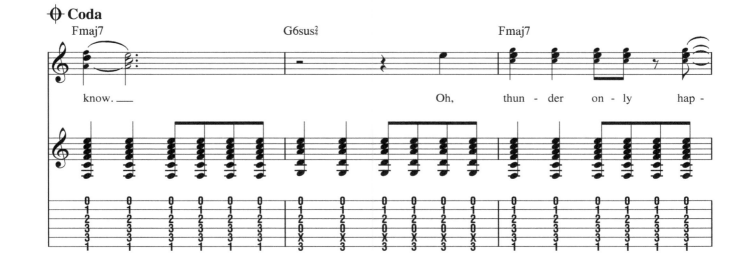

know. ___ Oh, thun - der on - ly hap-

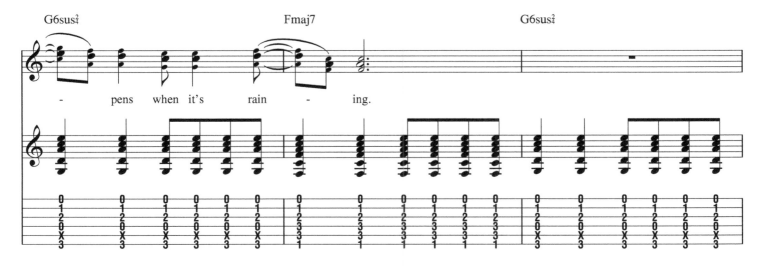

-pens when it's rain - ing.

Play - ers on - ly love _____ you when they're play - ing. _____

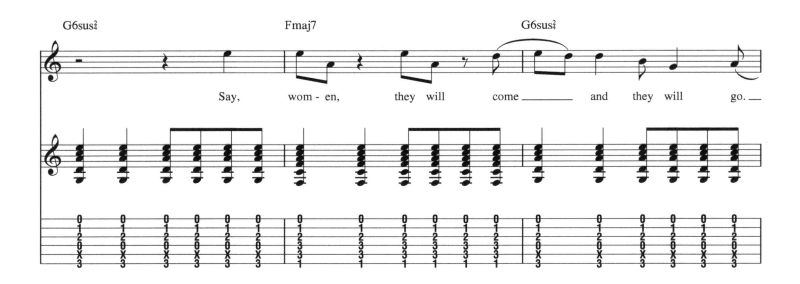

Say, wom - en, they will come _____ and they will go. ___

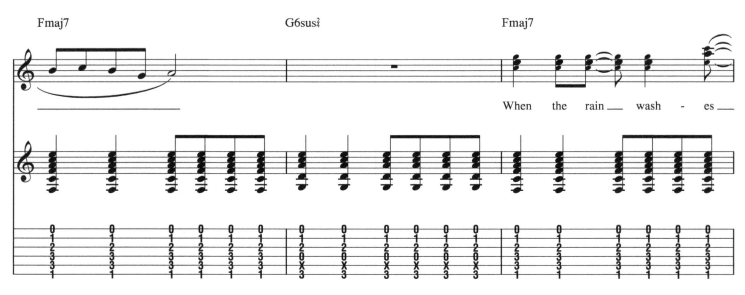

_____ When the rain ___ wash - es ___

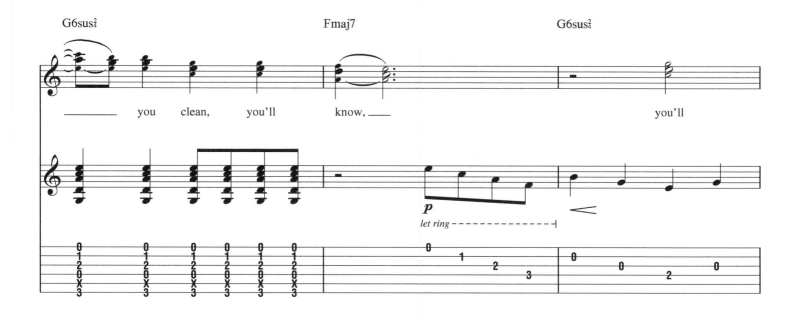

you clean, you'll know, _____ you'll

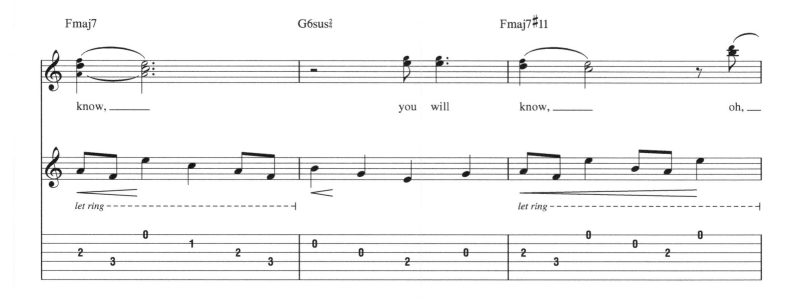

know, _____ you will know, _____ oh, _____

_____ oh, _____ oh, _____ you'll know. _____

Go Your Own Way

Words and Music by Lindsey Buckingham

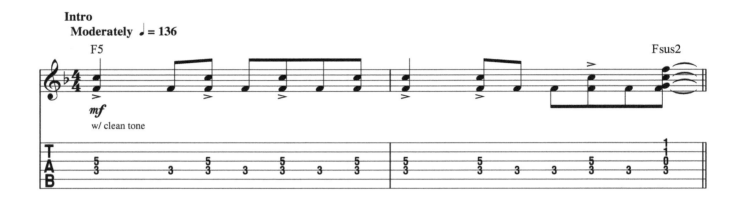

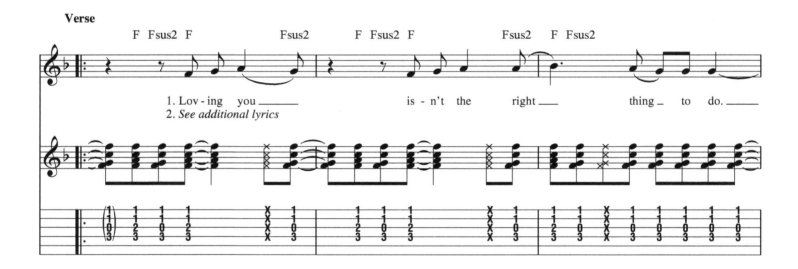

1. Lov-ing you _____ is-n't the right _____ thing _ to do. _____
2. *See additional lyrics*

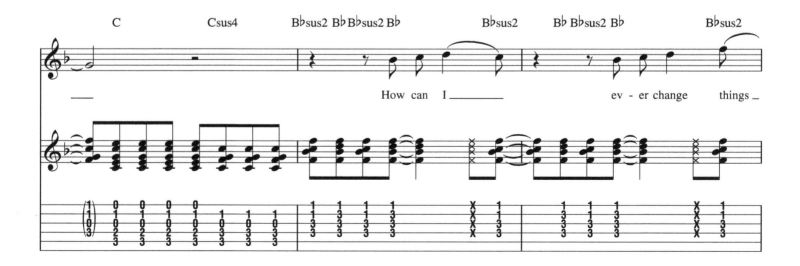

_____ How can I _____ ev - er change things _

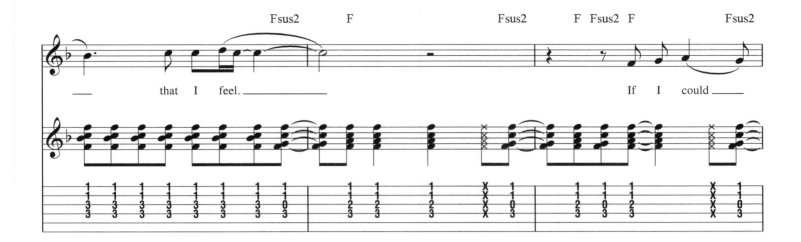

that I feel. _____ If I could _____

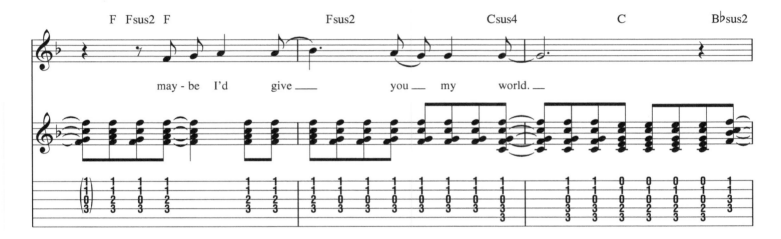

may - be I'd give _____ you ___ my world. _____

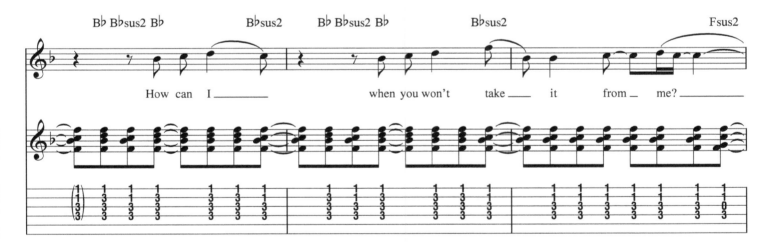

How can I _____ when you won't take _____ it from _ me? _____

𝄋 Chorus

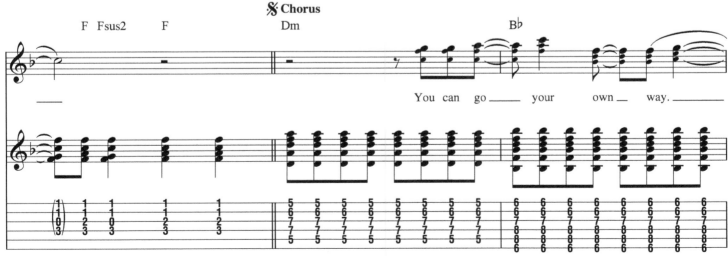

___ You can go _____ your own _ way. _____

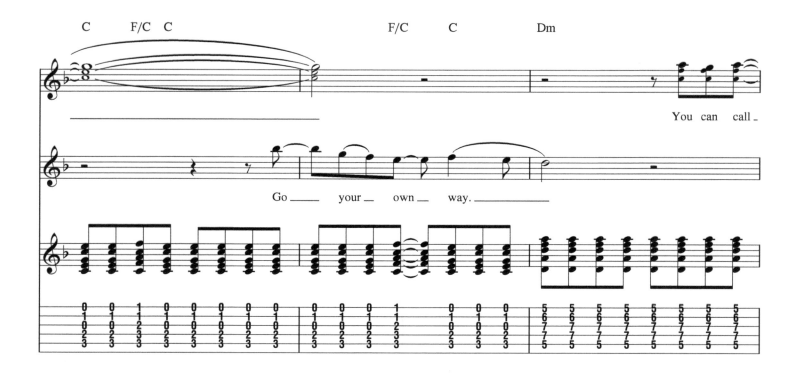

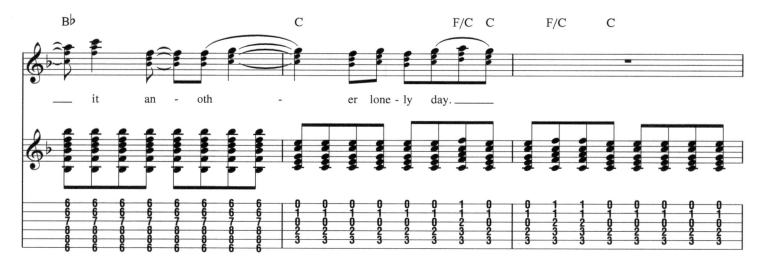

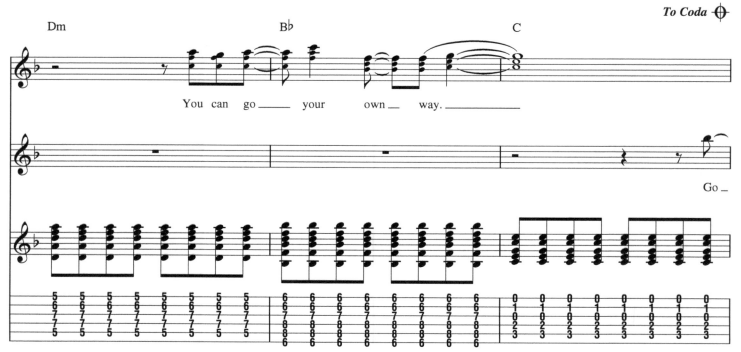

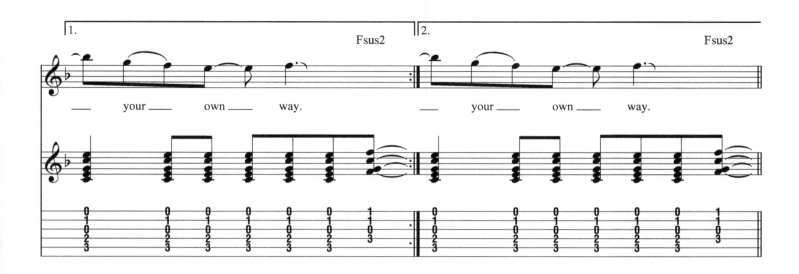

your — own — way.   — your — own — way.

Interlude

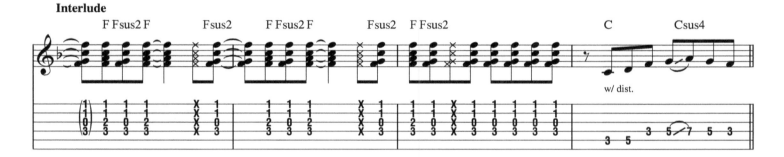

w/ dist.

Guitar Solo

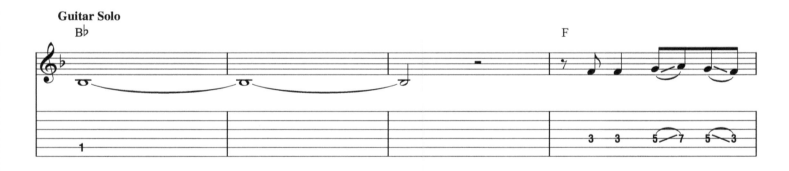

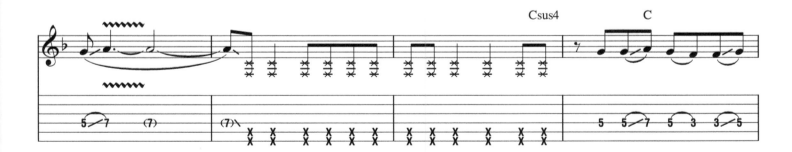

D.S. al Coda

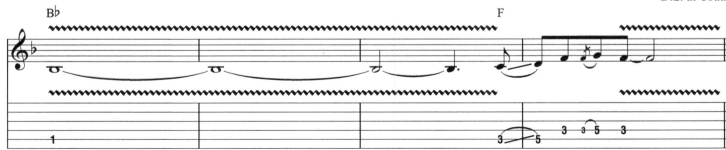

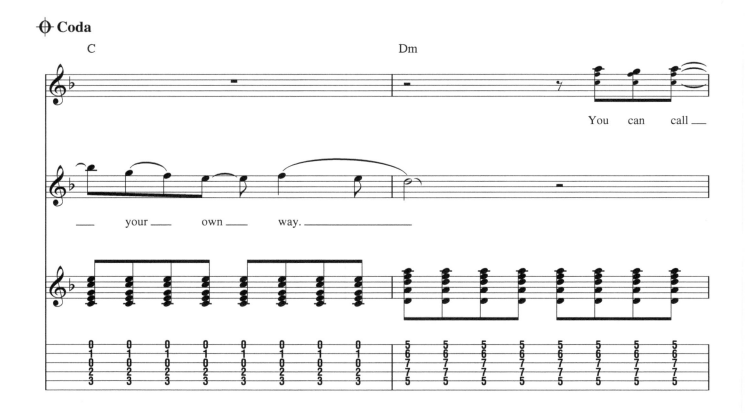

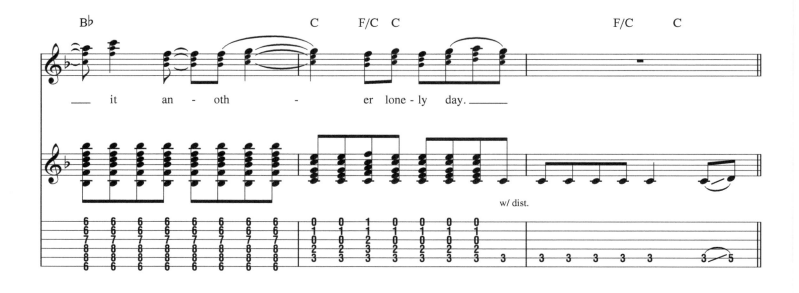

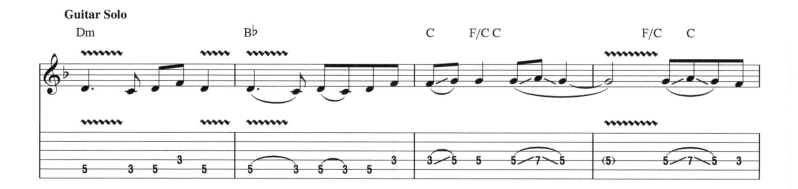

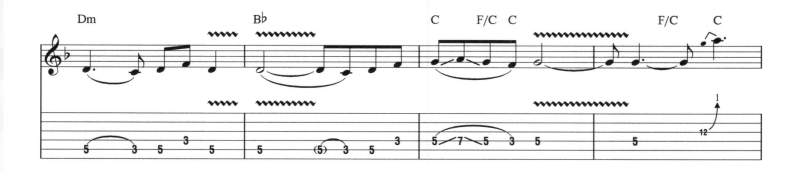

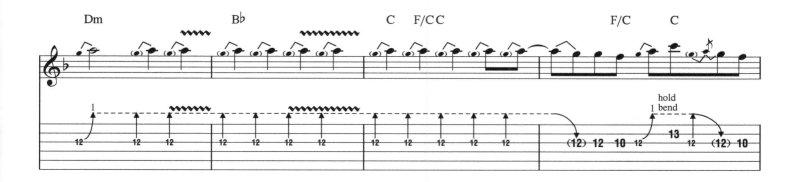

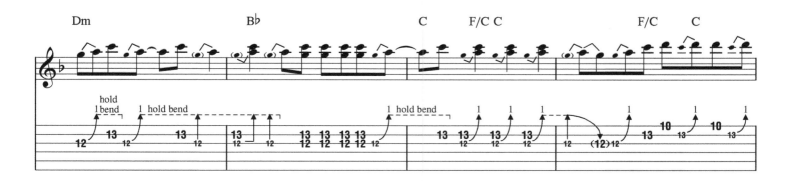

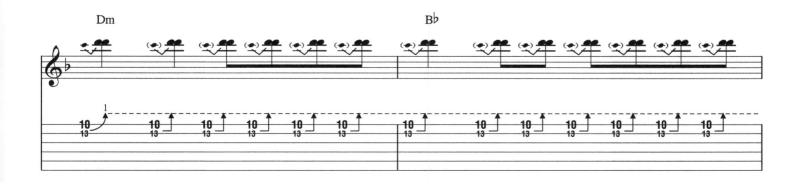

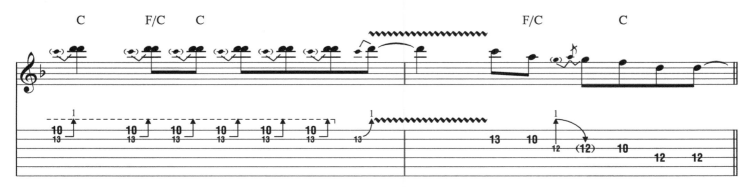

Outro-Chorus

You can go ___ your own ___ way. _____

Go ___

Begin fade

You can call ___ it an - oth -

your ___ own ___ way. _____

Fade out

- er lone - ly day. _____

Additional Lyrics

2. Tell me why ev'rything turned around.
Packin' up, shackin' up's all you wanna do.
If I could, baby, I'd give you my world.
Open up; ev'rything's waiting for you.

Rhiannon

Words and Music by Stevie Nicks

Takes to the sky ___ like a bird in flight. ___ And who will be ___ her lov-

Chorus

-er? All your life ___ you've nev - er seen ___ a wom - an ___

___ tak - en by the wind. ___ Would you stay ___ if she prom-

*T = thumb on 6th stg.

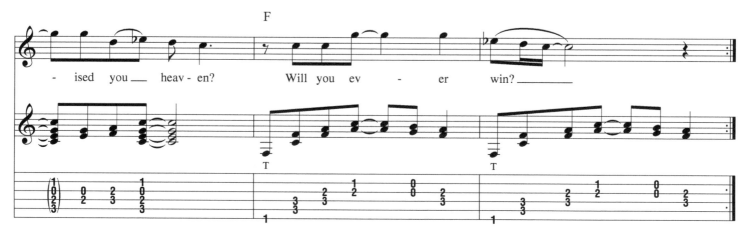

- ised you ___ heav - en? Will you ev - er win? ___

Interlude

Will you ev - er win? _____

Rhi -

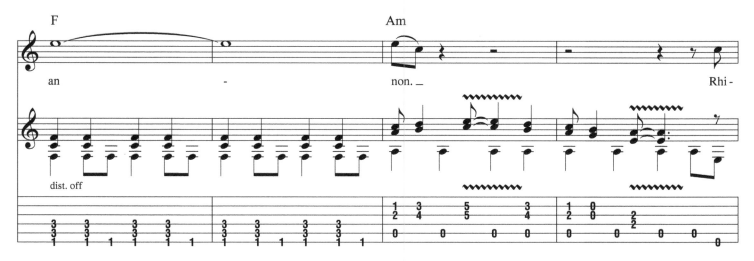

an - non. ___

Rhi -

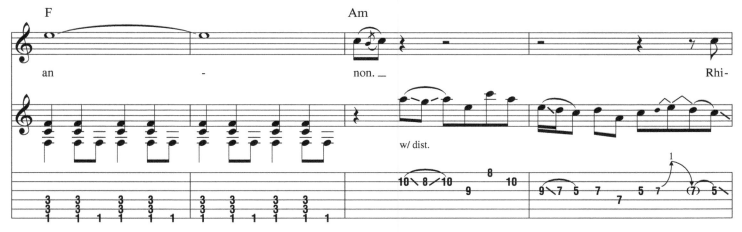

an - non. ___

Rhi -

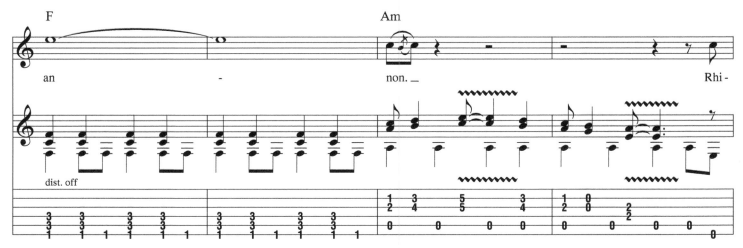

an - non. ___

Rhi -

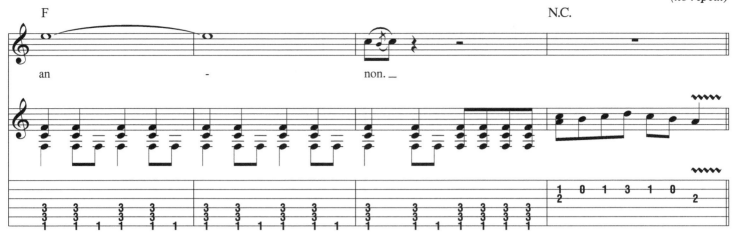

⊕ Coda

Interlude

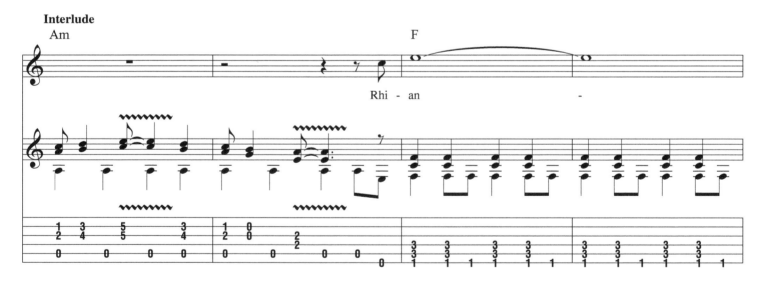

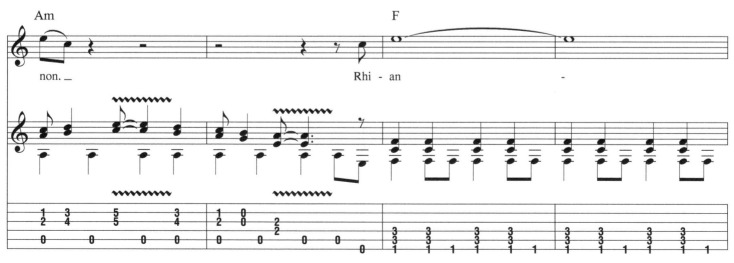

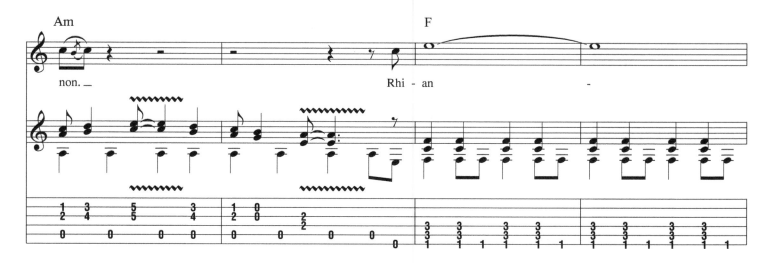

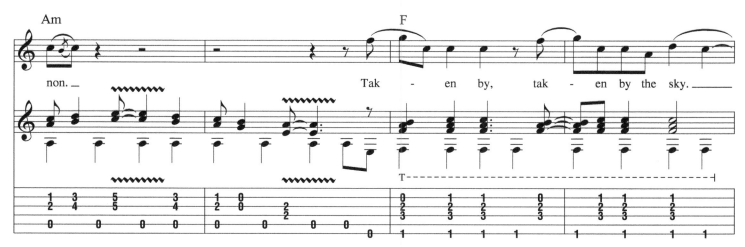

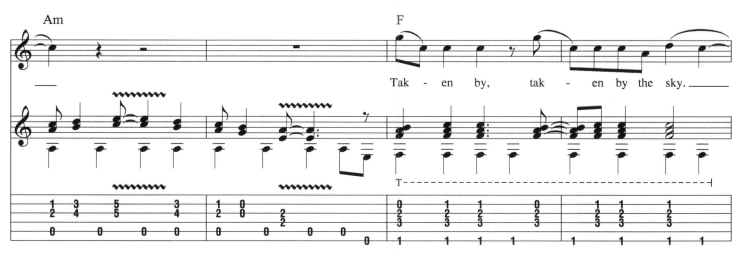

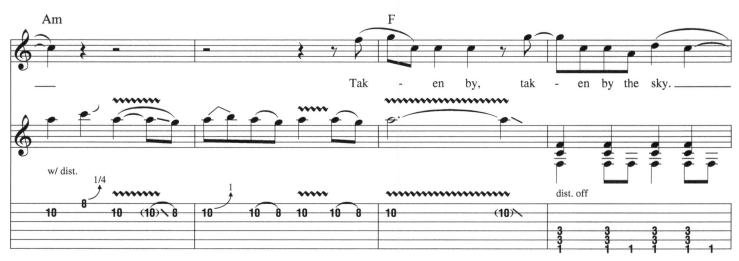

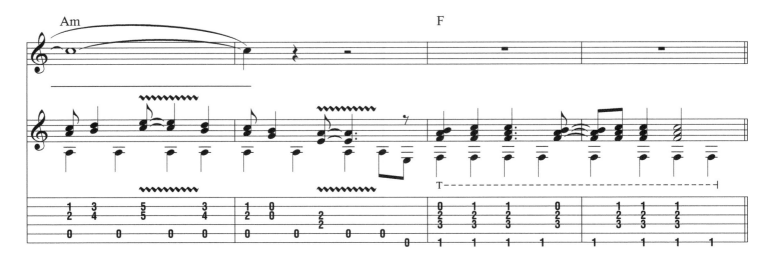

Outro-Guitar Solo

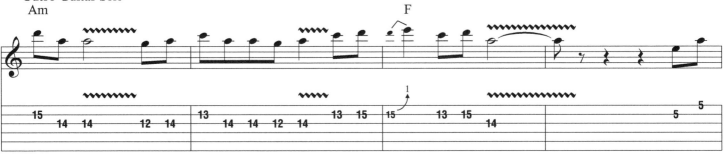

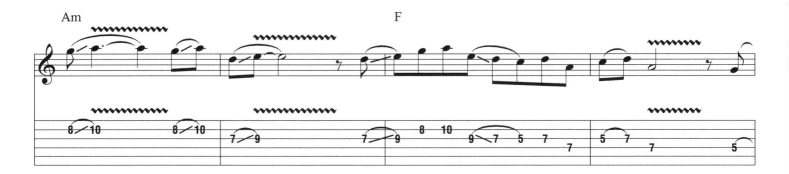

Begin fade

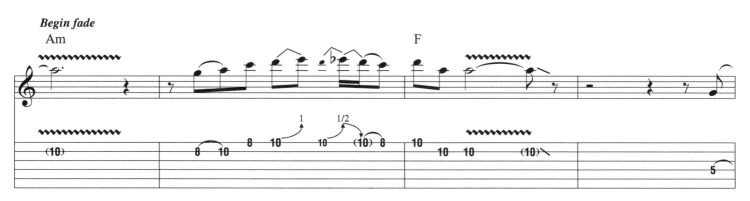

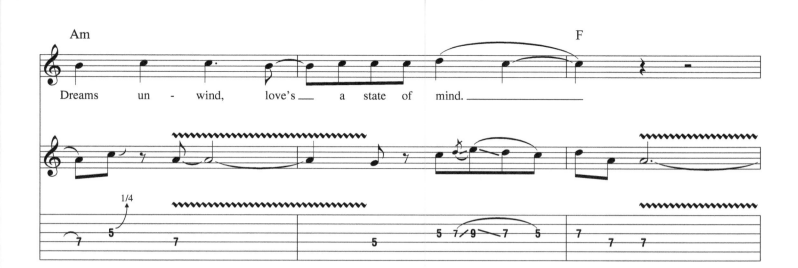

Dreams un - wind, love's __ a state of mind. _____

Dreams __ un - wind, love's __ a state of mind. _____

Fade out

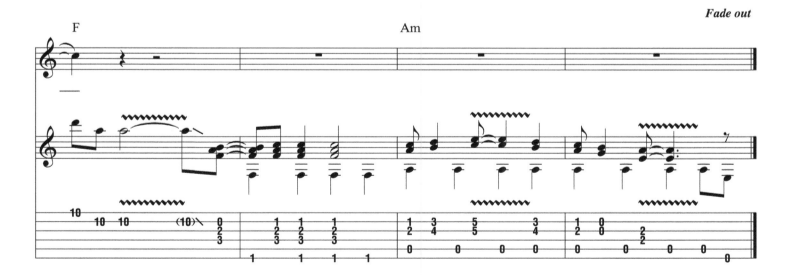

Additional Lyrics

2. She is like a cat in the dark.
   And then she is the darkness.
   She rules her life like a fine skylark.
   And when the sky is starless.

3. She rings like a bell through the night.
   And wouldn't you love to love her?
   She rules her life like a bird in flight.
   And who will be her lover?

Gold Dust Woman

Words and Music by Stevie Nicks

Double Drop D tuning:
(low to high) D-A-D-G-B-D

Intro
Moderately ♩ = 123

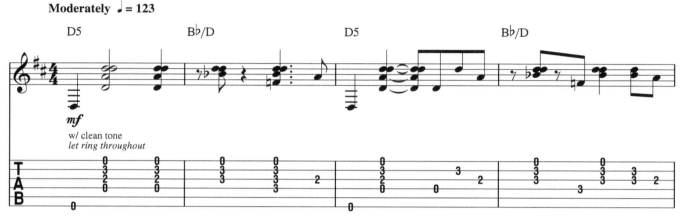

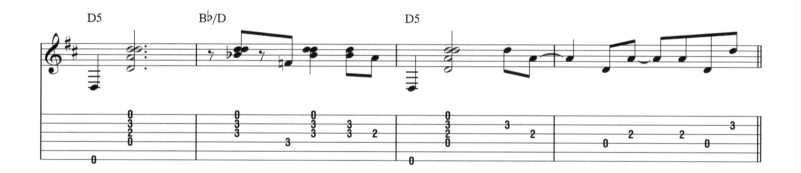

Verse

1. Rock on, __ gold dust wom-an. Take your sil - ver spoon; dig your __ grave. __

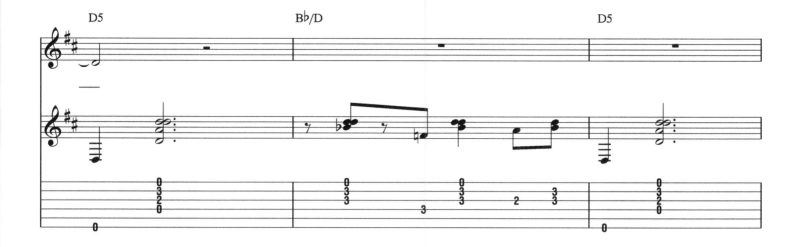

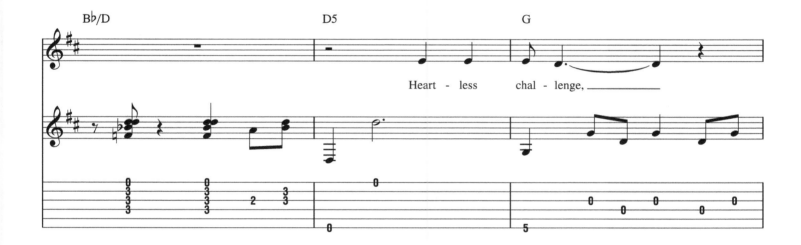

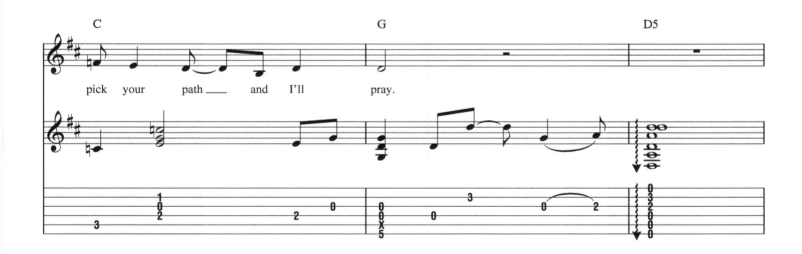

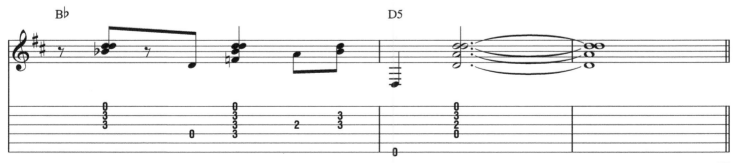

Verse

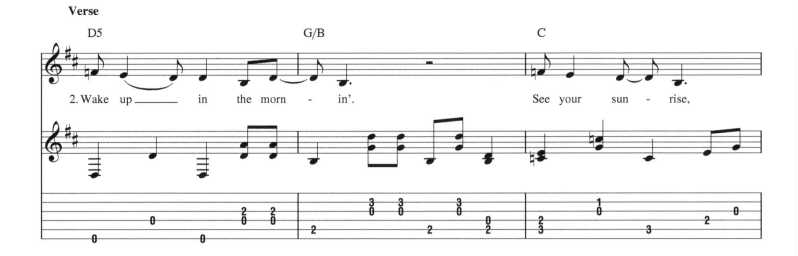

2. Wake up _____ in the morn - in'.   See your sun - rise,

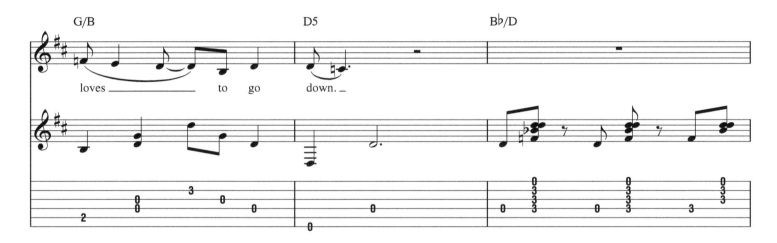

loves _____ to go down. ___

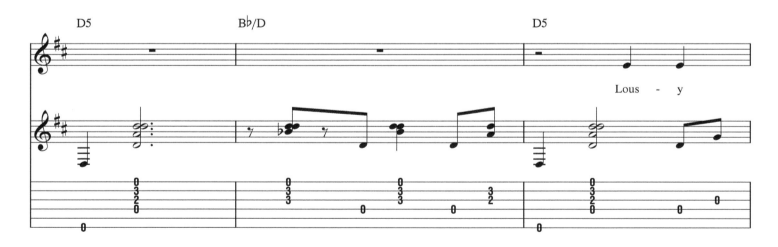

Lous - y

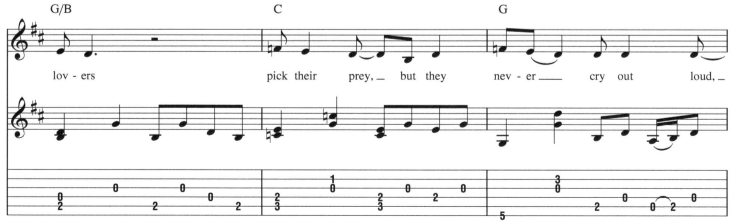

lov - ers   pick their prey, __ but they   nev - er ___ cry out loud, __

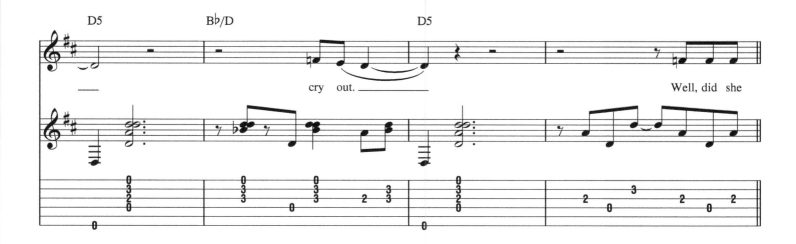

cry out. _____ Well, did she

Chorus

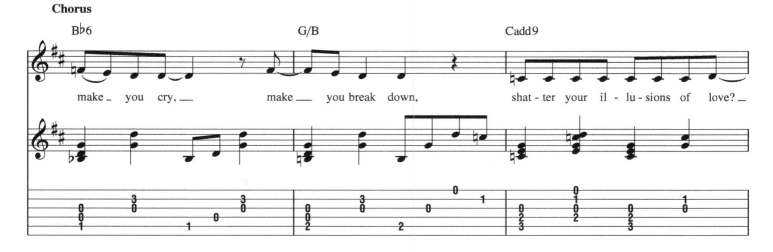

make _ you cry, ___ make ___ you break down, shat - ter your il - lu - sions of love? __

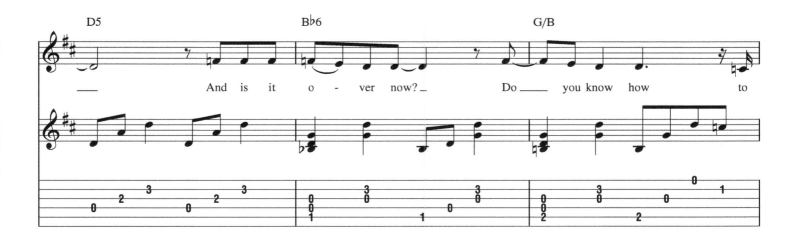

_ And is it o - ver now? _ Do ___ you know how to

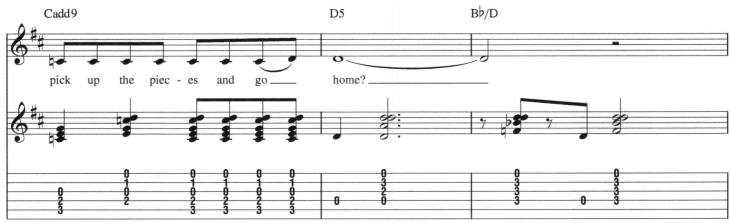

pick up the piec - es and go ___ home? _____

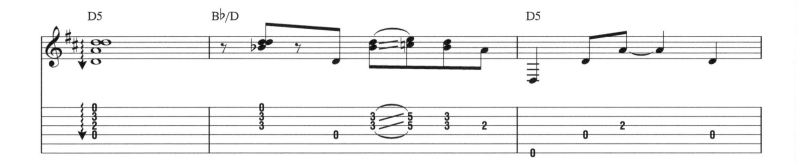

Verse

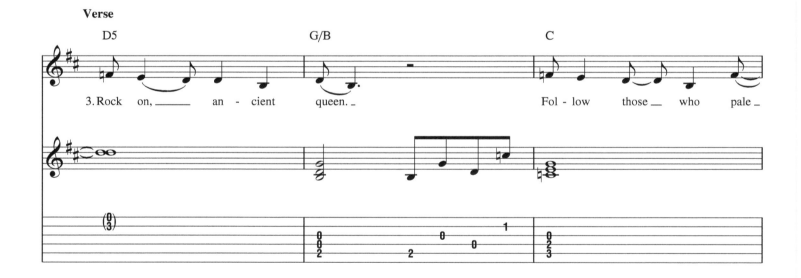

3. Rock on, _____ an - cient queen. _____ Fol - low those _____ who pale _____

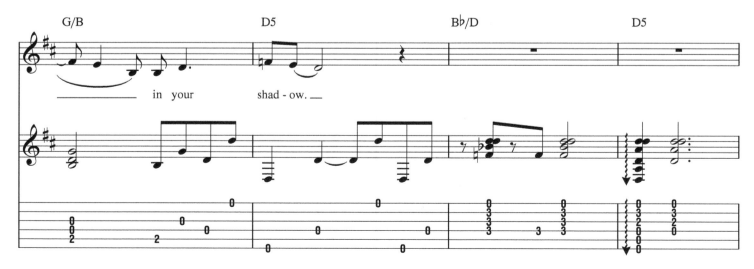

_____ in your shad - ow. _____

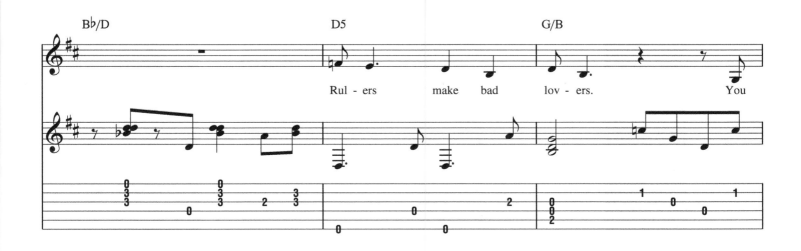

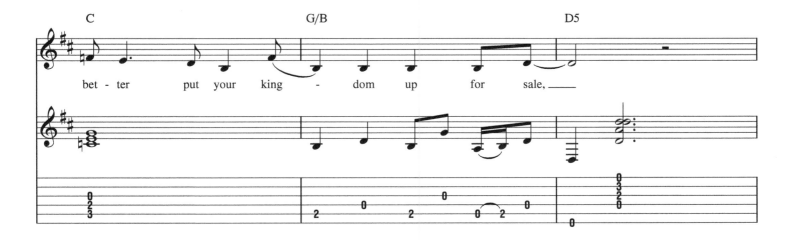

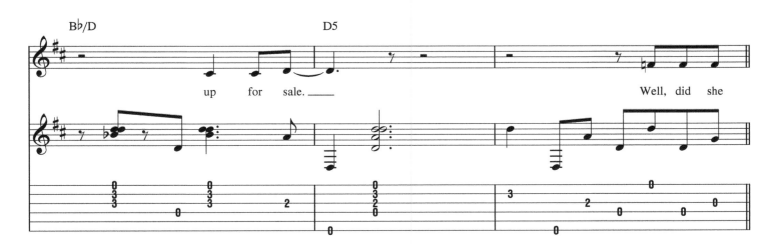

Chorus

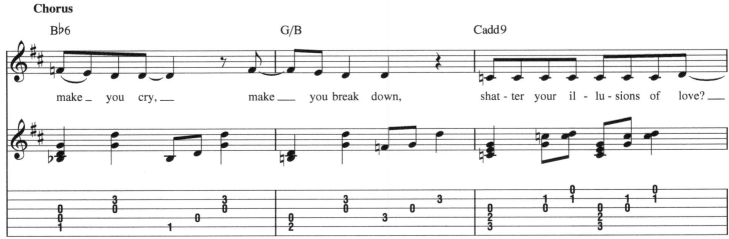

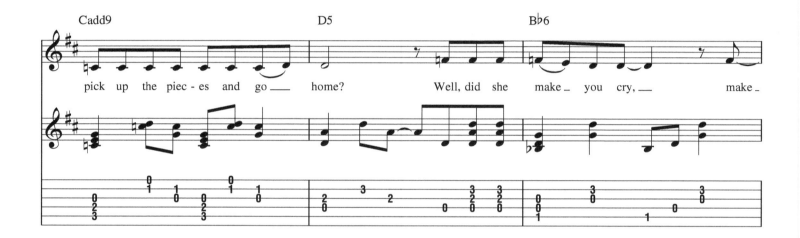

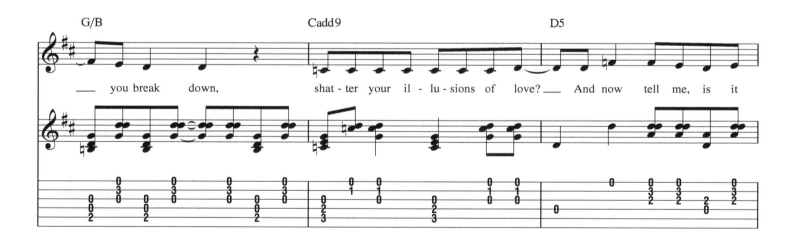

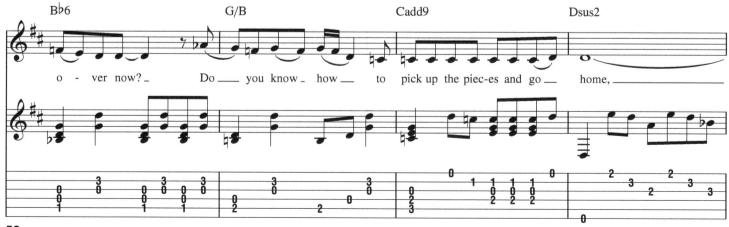

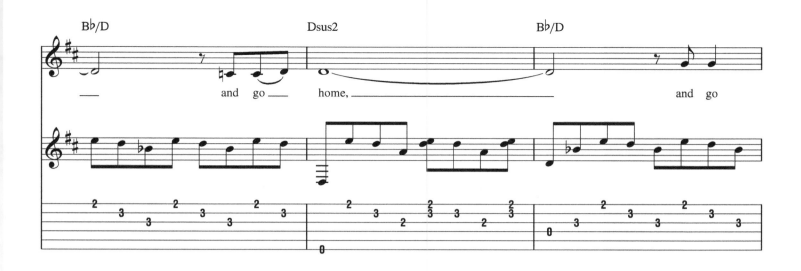

and go home,   and go

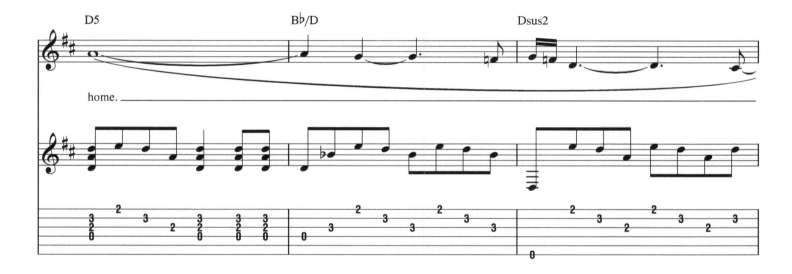

home.

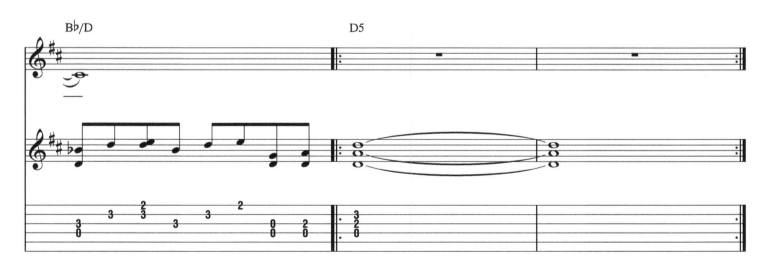

Outro

Repeat and fade

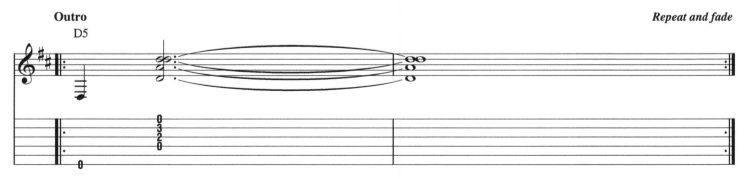

Never Going Back Again

Words and Music by Lindsey Buckingham

Drop D tuning, Capo IV:
(low to high) D-A-D-G-B-E

Intro
Moderately ♩ = 88

F#
*(D)

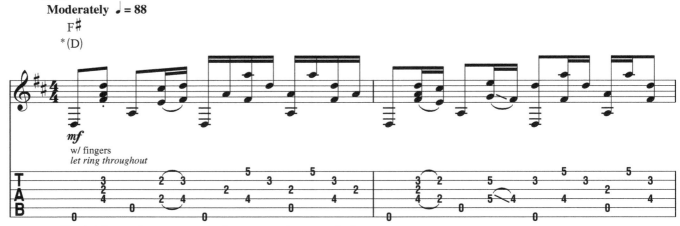

*Symbols in parentheses represent chord names respective to capoed guitar.
Symbols above reflect actual sounding chords. Capoed fret is "0" in tab.

C#13(no3rd)
(A13(no3rd))   F#
                                                                            (D)

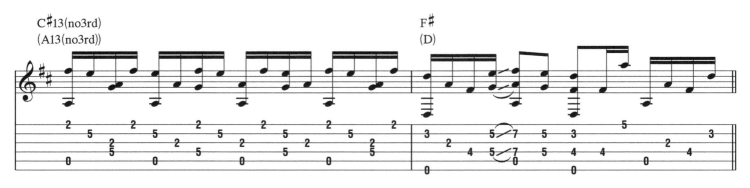

 Verse

F#
(D)

1. She broke down____ and let   me __ in. __
2. *See additional lyrics*

C#13(no3rd)
(A13(no3rd))   F#
                                                                            (D)

Made me _ see where I've _ been. _____

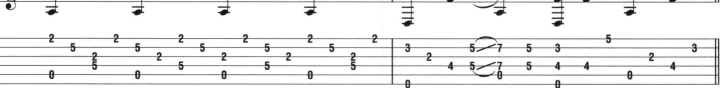

C#13(no3rd)
(A13(no3rd))

F#
(D)

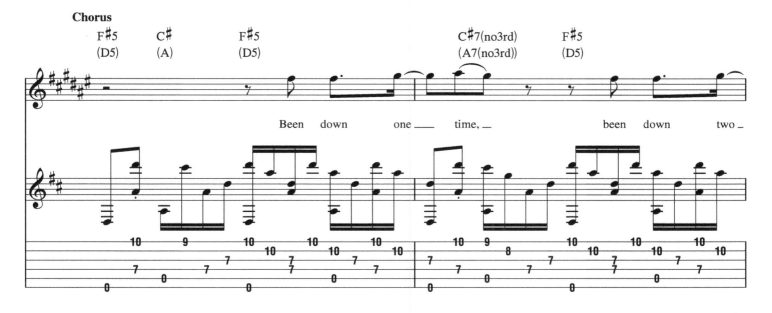

Chorus

F#5   C#   F#5   C#7(no3rd)   F#5

(D5)   (A)   (D5)   (A7(no3rd))   (D5)

Been down one _ time, _   been down two _

To Coda ⊕

C#   F#5   D#m   A#m7   D#m   C#

(A)   (D5)   (Bm)   (F#m7)   (Bm)   (A)

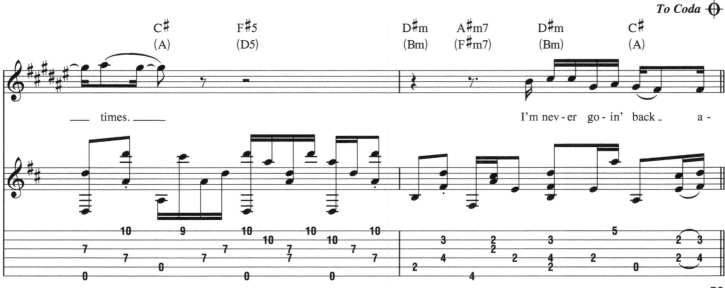

_ times. _____   I'm nev-er go-in' back _ a-

Interlude

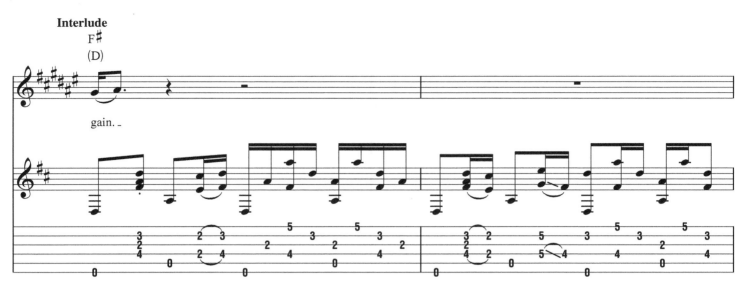

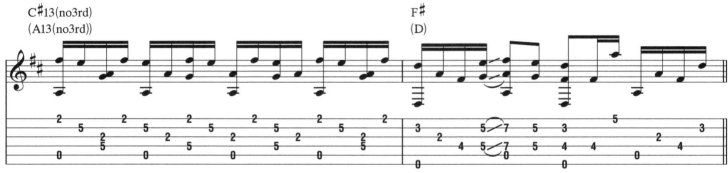

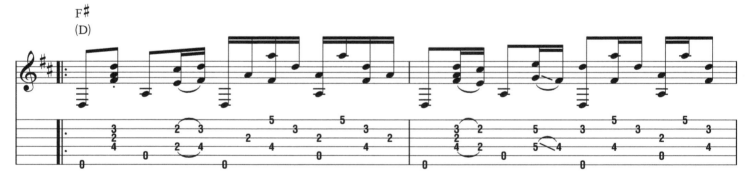

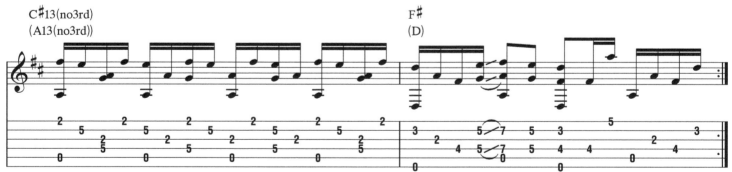

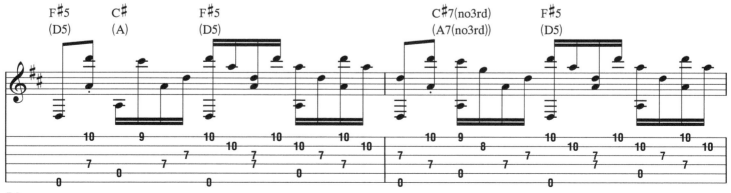

Mm. _____

Coda

Outro

Additional Lyrics

2. You don't know what it means to win.
Come down and see me again.

You Make Lovin' Fun

Words and Music by Christine McVie

Intro
Moderately ♩ = 126

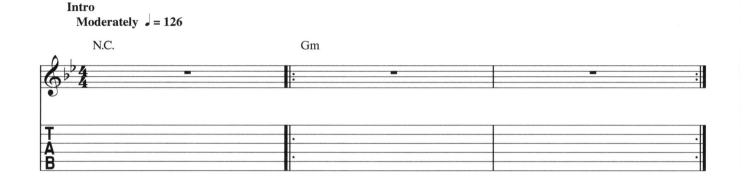

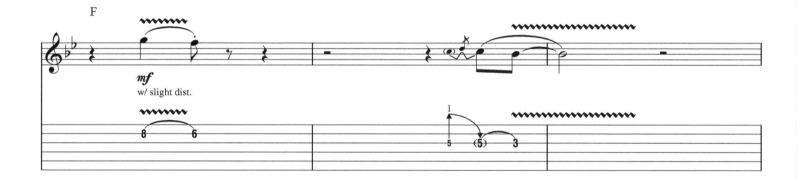

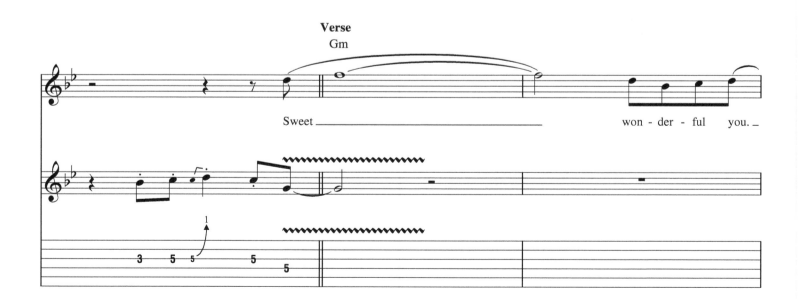

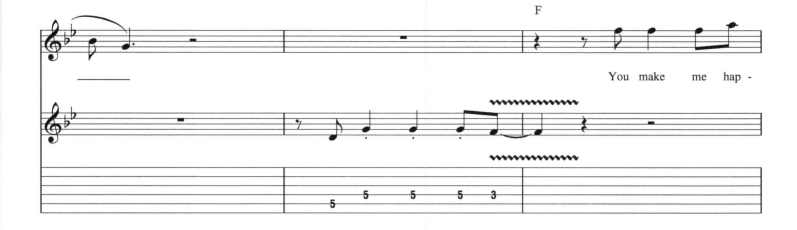

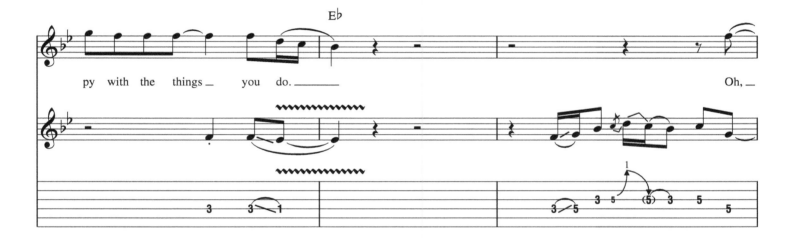

Chorus
Half-time feel

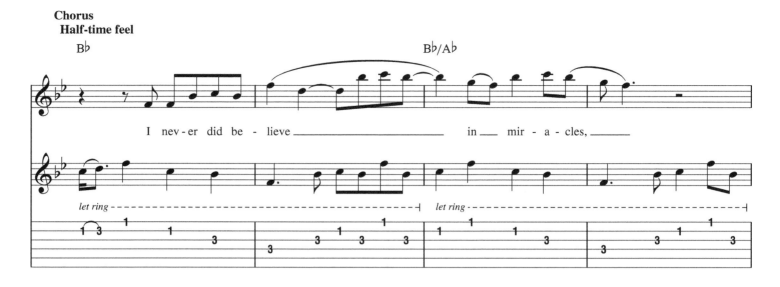

I nev-er did be-lieve _____ in ____ mir - a - cles, _____

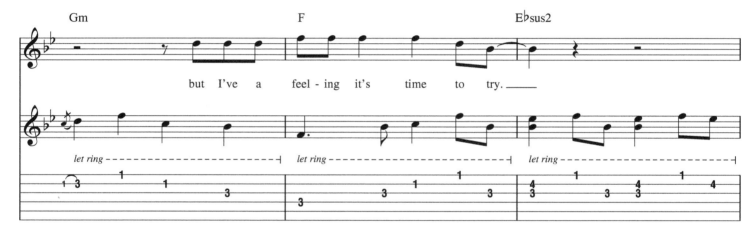

but I've a feel - ing it's time to try. _____

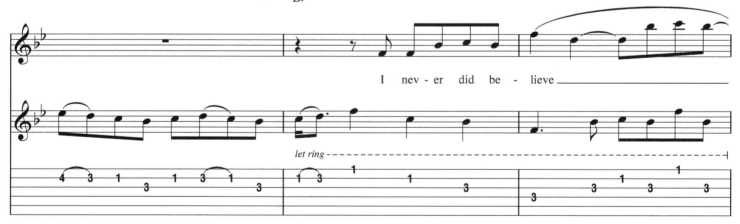

I nev - er did be - lieve _____

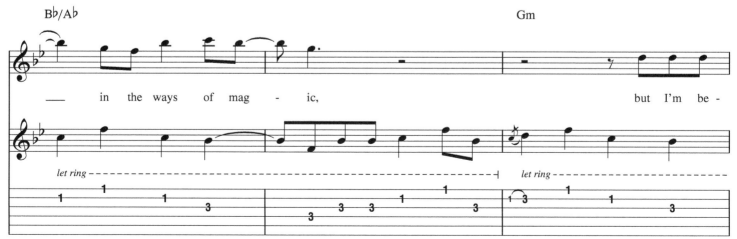

_____ in the ways of mag - ic, but I'm be -

End half-time feel

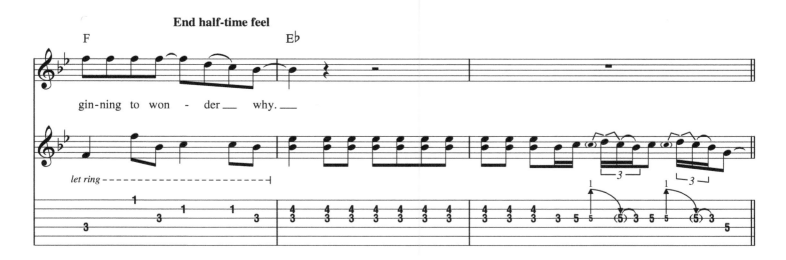

gin-ning to won - der — why. —

Guitar Solo

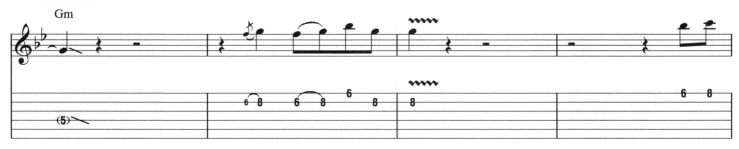

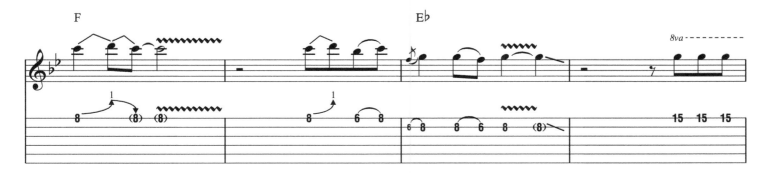

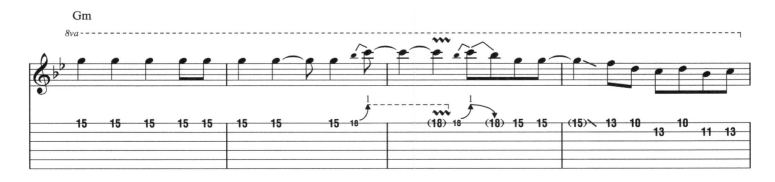

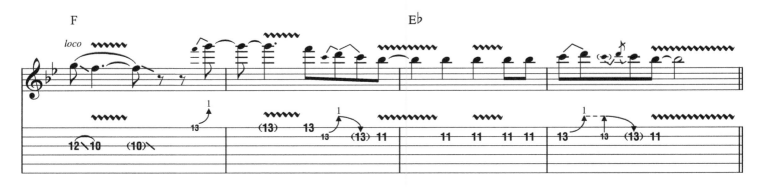

Verse

don't _ break the spell. _____

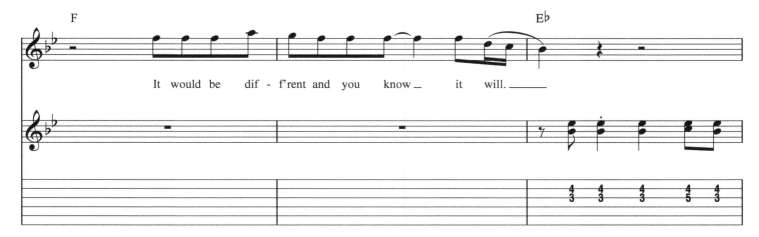

It would be dif - f'rent and you know _ it will. _____

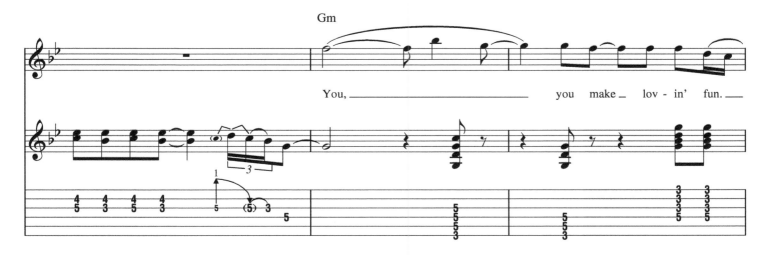

You, _____ you make _ lov - in' fun. _

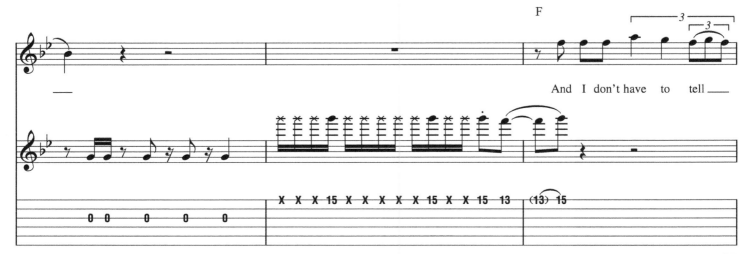

And I don't have to tell _____

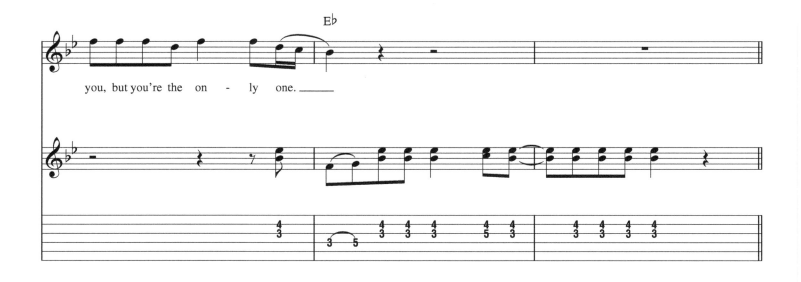

you, but you're the on - ly one. ____

Outro-Chorus

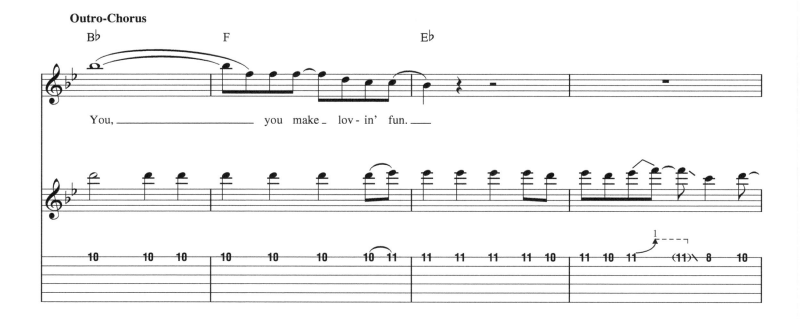

You, _____ you make _ lov - in' fun. ____

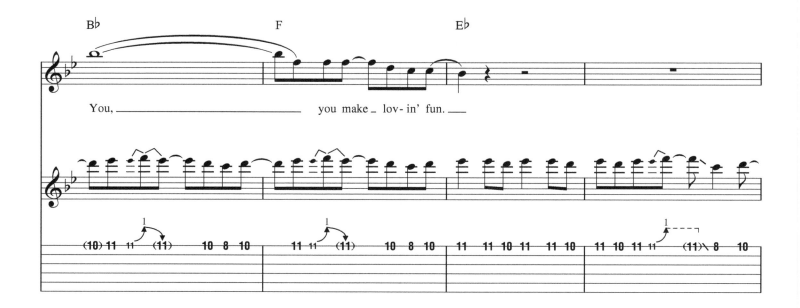

You, _____ you make _ lov - in' fun. ____

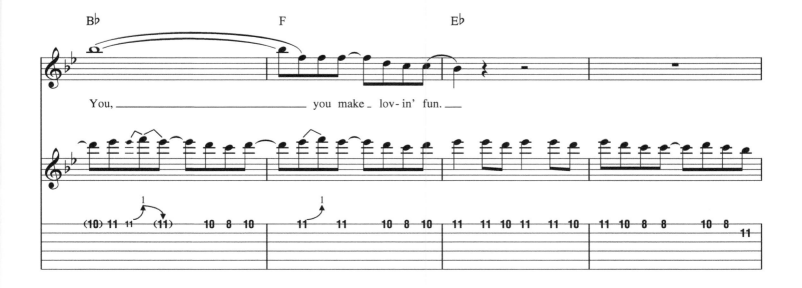

You, _____ you make _ lov- in' fun. __

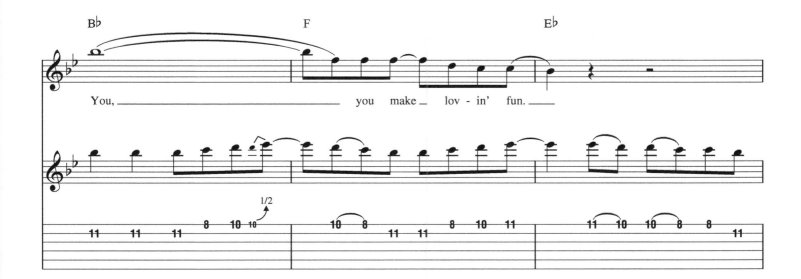

You, _____ you make _ lov - in' fun. __

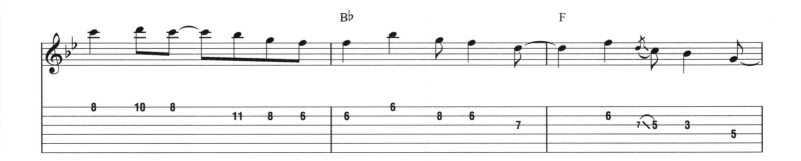

GUITAR NOTATION LEGEND

THE MUSICAL STAFF shows pitches and rhythms and is divided by bar lines into measures. Pitches are named after the first seven letters of the alphabet.

TABLATURE graphically represents the guitar fingerboard. Each horizontal line represents a string, and each number represents a fret.

4th string, 2nd fret   1st & 2nd strings open, played together   open D chord

HALF-STEP BEND: Strike the note and bend up 1/2 step.

WHOLE-STEP BEND: Strike the note and bend up one step.

GRACE NOTE BEND: Strike the note and immediately bend up as indicated.

SLIGHT (MICROTONE) BEND: Strike the note and bend up 1/4 step.

BEND AND RELEASE: Strike the note and bend up as indicated, then release back to the original note. Only the first note is struck.

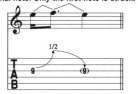

PRE-BEND: Bend the note as indicated, then strike it.

VIBRATO: The string is vibrated by rapidly bending and releasing the note with the fretting hand.

PALM MUTING: The note is partially muted by the pick hand lightly touching the string(s) just before the bridge.

HAMMER-ON: Strike the first (lower) note with one finger, then sound the higher note (on the same string) with another finger by fretting it without picking.

PULL-OFF: Place both fingers on the notes to be sounded. Strike the first note and without picking, pull the finger off to sound the second (lower) note.

LEGATO SLIDE: Strike the first note and then slide the same fret-hand finger up or down to the second note. The second note is not struck.

SHIFT SLIDE: Same as legato slide, except the second note is struck.

TRILL: Very rapidly alternate between the notes indicated by continuously hammering on and pulling off.

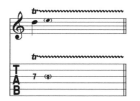

TAPPING: Hammer ("tap") the fret indicated with the pick-hand index or middle finger and pull off to the note fretted by the fret hand.

NATURAL HARMONIC: Strike the note while the fret-hand lightly touches the string directly over the fret indicated.

Harm.

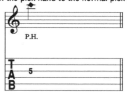

PINCH HARMONIC: The note is fretted normally and a harmonic is produced by adding the edge of the thumb or the tip of the index finger of the pick hand to the normal pick attack.

P.H.

TREMOLO PICKING: The note is picked as rapidly and continuously as possible.

VIBRATO BAR DIVE AND RETURN: The pitch of the note or chord is dropped a specified number of steps (in rhythm), then returned to the original pitch.

w/ bar

VIBRATO BAR SCOOP: Depress the bar just before striking the note, then quickly release the bar.

w/ bar

VIBRATO BAR DIP: Strike the note and then immediately drop a specified number of steps, then release back to the original pitch.

w/ bar

Additional Musical Definitions

 (accent) • Accentuate note (play it louder).

 (staccato) • Play the note short.

D.S. al Coda • Go back to the sign (𝄋), then play until the measure marked "***To Coda***," then skip to the section labelled "**Coda**."

D.C. al Fine • Go back to the beginning of the song and play until the measure marked "***Fine***" (end).

Fill • Label used to identify a brief melodic figure which is to be inserted into the arrangement.

N.C. • Harmony is implied.

 • Repeat measures between signs.

 • When a repeated section has different endings, play the first ending only the first time and the second ending only the second time.